A RETREAT WITH LUKE

Other titles in the A Retreat With... *Series:*

A RETREAT WITH LUKE

Stepping Out on the Word of God

Barbara E. Reid, O.P.

ST. ANTHONY MESSENGER PRESS

Cincinnati, Ohio

Scripture citations are taken from the *New Revised Standard Version Bible,* copyright ©1989 by the Division of Christian Education of the National Council of Churches of Christ in the U.S.A. and used by permission.

We are grateful for permission to quote material printed by the following publishers:

Reprinted by permission of Orbis Books, excerpts from *Parables, Arrows of God,* by Megan McKenna, copyright ©1994. Reprinted by permission of Benetvision, "A Litany of Women for the Church," by Sister Joan D. Chittister, O.S.B., copyright Benedictine Sisters of Erie. Reprinted by permission of The Oregon Catholic Press, "Take, Lord, Receive," by John Foley, copyright ©1975. Reprinted by permission of Loyola Press, excerpts from *The Gift of Peace,* by Joseph Cardinal Bernardin, copyright ©1997. Reprinted by permission of Forest of Peace Books, Inc., "Psalm of Pardon," by Edward Hays, copyright ©1988. Reprinted by permission of Continuum Publishing Group, excerpts from *Jesus: Miriam's Child, Sophia's Prophet,* by Elisabeth Schüssler Fiorenza, copyright ©1994. Reprinted by permission of Image Books, excerpt from *The Song of the Bird,* by Anthony DeMello, copyright ©1984. Reprinted by permission of Random House, excerpts from *Wouldn't Take Nothing For My Journey Now,* by Maya Angelou, copyright ©1993. Reprinted by permission of Farrar, Straus & Giroux, Inc., excerpt from "Revelation," from *Complete Stories,* by Flannery O'Connor, copyright ©1971. Reprinted by permission of Twenty-Third Publications, "A Litany of Women's Power," from *Women's Prayer Services,* by Iben Gjerding and Katherine Kinnamon, copyright ©1987. Reprinted by permission of Penguin Putnam, excerpt from *A Raisin in the Sun,* by Lorraine Hansberry, copyright ©1959.

Cover illustration by Steve Erspamer, S.M.
Cover and book design by Mary Alfieri
Electronic format and pagination by Sandy L. Digman

ISBN 0-86716-332-1

Copyright ©2000, Barbara E. Reid, O.P.

Published by St. Anthony Messenger Press
www.AmericanCatholic.org
Printed in the U.S.A.

Contents

Introducing A Retreat With...

Twenty years ago I made a weekend retreat at a Franciscan house on the coast of New Hampshire. The retreat director's opening talk was as lively as a long-range weather forecast. He told us how completely God loves each one of us—without benefit of lively anecdotes or fresh insights.

As the friar rambled on, my inner critic kept up a *sotto voce* commentary: "I've heard all this before." "Wish he'd say something new that I could chew on." "That poor man really doesn't have much to say." Ever hungry for manna yet untasted, I devalued any experience of hearing the same old thing.

After a good night's sleep, I awoke feeling as peaceful as a traveler who has at last arrived safely home. I walked across the room toward the closet. On the way I passed the sink with its small framed mirror on the wall above. Something caught my eye like an unexpected presence. I turned, saw the reflection in the mirror and said aloud, "No wonder he loves me!"

This involuntary affirmation stunned me. What or whom had I seen in the mirror? When I looked again, it was "just me," an ordinary person with a lower-than-average reservoir of self-esteem. But I knew that in the initial vision I had seen God-in-me breaking through like a sudden sunrise.

At that moment I knew what it meant to be made in the divine image. I understood right down to my size eleven feet what it meant to be loved exactly as I was.

Only later did I connect this revelation with one granted to the Trappist monk-writer Thomas Merton. As he reports in *Conjectures of a Guilty Bystander*, while standing all unsuspecting on a street corner one day, he was overwhelmed by the "joy of being...a member of a race in which God Himself became incarnate.... There is no way of telling people that they are all walking around shining like the sun."

As an absentminded homemaker may leave a wedding ring on the kitchen windowsill, so I have often mislaid this precious conviction. But I have never forgotten that particular retreat. It persuaded me that the Spirit rushes in where it will. Not even a boring director or a judgmental retreatant can withstand the "violent wind" that "fills the entire house" where we dwell in expectation (see Acts 2:2).

So why deny ourselves any opportunity to come aside awhile and rest on holy ground? Why not withdraw from the daily web that keeps us muddled and wound? Wordsworth's complaint is ours as well: "The world is too much with us." There is no flu shot to protect us from infection by the skepticism of the media, the greed of commerce, the alienating influence of technology. We need retreats as the deer needs the running stream.

An Invitation

This book and its companions in the *A Retreat With...* series from St. Anthony Messenger Press are designed to meet that need. They are an invitation to choose as director some of the most powerful, appealing and wise mentors our faith tradition has to offer.

Our directors come from many countries, historical eras and schools of spirituality. At times they are teamed to sing in close harmony (for example, Francis de Sales, Jane de Chantal and Aelred of Rievaulx on spiritual friendship). Others are paired to kindle an illuminating fire from the friction of their differing views (such as Augustine of Hippo and Mary Magdalene on human sexuality). All have been chosen because, in their humanness and their holiness, they can help us grow in self-knowledge, discernment of God's will and maturity in the Spirit.

Inviting us into relationship with these saints and holy ones are inspired authors from today's world, women and men whose creative gifts open our windows to the Spirit's flow. As a motto for the authors of our series, we have borrowed the advice of Dom Frederick Dunne to the young Thomas Merton. Upon joining the Trappist monks, Merton wanted to sacrifice his writing activities lest they interfere with his contemplative vocation. Dom Frederick wisely advised, "Keep on writing books that make people love the spiritual life."

That is our motto. Our purpose is to foster (or strengthen) friendships between readers and retreat directors—friendships that feed the soul with wisdom, past and present. Like the scribe "trained for the kingdom of heaven," each author brings forth from his or her storeroom "what is new and what is old" (Matthew 13:52).

The Format

The pattern for each *A Retreat With...* remains the same; readers of one will be in familiar territory when they move on to the next. Each book is organized as a seven-session retreat that readers may adapt to their own schedules or to the needs of a group.

Day One begins with an anecdotal introduction called "Getting to Know Our Directors." Readers are given a telling glimpse of the guides with whom they will be sharing the retreat experience. A second section, "Placing Our Directors in Context," will enable retreatants to see the guides in their own historical, geographical, cultural and spiritual settings.

Having made the human link between seeker and guide, the authors go on to "Introducing Our Retreat Theme." This section clarifies how the guide(s) are especially suited to explore the theme and how the retreatant's spirituality can be nourished by it.

After an original "Opening Prayer" to breathe life into the day's reflection, the author, speaking with and through the mentor(s), will begin to spin out the theme. While focusing on the guide(s)' own words and experience, the author may also draw on Scripture, tradition, literature, art, music, psychology or contemporary events to illuminate the path.

Each day's session is followed by reflection questions designed to challenge, affirm and guide the reader in integrating the theme into daily life. A "Closing Prayer" brings the session full circle and provides a spark of inspiration for the reader to harbor until the next session.

Days Two through Six begin with "Coming Together in the Spirit" and follow a format similar to Day One. Day Seven weaves the entire retreat together, encourages a continuation of the mentoring relationship and concludes with "Deepening Your Acquaintance," an envoi to live the theme by God's grace, the director(s)' guidance and the retreatant's discernment. A closing section of Resources serves as a larder from which readers may draw enriching books, videos, cassettes and films.

We hope readers will experience at least one of those memorable "No wonder God loves me!" moments. And we hope that they will have "talked back" to the mentors, as good friends are wont to do.

A case in point: There was once a famous preacher who always drew a capacity crowd to the cathedral. Whenever he spoke, an eccentric old woman sat in the front pew directly beneath the pulpit. She took every opportunity to mumble complaints and contradictions— just loud enough for the preacher to catch the drift that he was not as wonderful as he was reputed to be. Others seated down front glowered at the woman and tried to shush her. But she went right on needling the preacher to her heart's content.

When the old woman died, the congregation was astounded at the depth and sincerity of the preacher's grief. Asked why he was so bereft, he responded, "Now who will help me to grow?"

All of our mentors in *A Retreat With...* are worthy guides. Yet none would seek retreatants who simply said, "Where you lead, I will follow. You're the expert." In truth, our directors provide only half the retreat's content. Readers themselves will generate the other half.

As general editor for the retreat series, I pray that readers will, by their questions, comments, doubts and decision-making, fertilize the seeds our mentors have planted.

And may the Spirit of God rush in to give the growth.

Gloria Hutchinson
Series Editor
Conversion of Saint Paul, 1995

Getting to Know Our Director

I have always loved the Gospel of Luke. Each of the four Gospels has its own beauty, but I have always been most moved by the Third Gospel. The lovely opening chapters, with the Annunciations of the births of John the Baptist and Jesus, are found only in Luke. I am intrigued by the puzzling parables, and Luke tells more of them than any other evangelist. Luke's Gospel also has a particular emphasis on the poor and downtrodden and the inclusion in God's realm of such folks as Zacchaeus, and the woman who poured out ointment and tears on Jesus' feet out of love. This Gospel also has a focus on forgiveness and reconciliation. Only in Luke are the powerful stories of the lost and found "prodigal son" and the woman searching for a stray coin. There are more meals in Luke than the other Gospels, but I have always mused how Eucharistic overtones give way to indigestion—something controversial always happens when Jesus is coming to dinner!

Finally, as a woman biblical scholar I have been attracted to the Third Gospel because it has more stories than the others that feature women characters. As we struggle in our own day for greater inclusivity and justice in our world and in the Church, I have found Luke's Gospel an indispensable companion on the way. I hope that as I try to open up these themes from the Gospel that this retreat may deepen your relationship with the Lucan Jesus and that the Spirit will guide you in Christ's way.

I hope you will indulge in some imaginative

reconstruction with me as I try to allow the evangelist and the characters from the Gospel to speak directly to you in their words. I would like to begin by introducing you to the evangelist, Luke. If we could cross the barriers of time and space and speak with him directly, these are some of the answers I think he might give us.

Q: Saint Luke, how did you first come to know about Jesus?

A: As you know from reading my prologue (Luke 1:1-4), I didn't know Jesus personally during his life on earth. But I've heard all the stories about Jesus from those who did and I feel as if I were there. I first heard of him when some of his followers came here preaching in Antioch. At that time I had been attracted to the Jewish faith. I had started reading their Scriptures and praying in their synagogue. There were a number of us Gentiles whom they called "God-fearers," that is, we didn't go all the way to become full members and be circumcised. Nor did we observe all their dietary regulations. It was a satisfactory relationship for me.

One day, a group of Jews visiting from Palestine got up to speak in the synagogue. They told amazing stories about a man named Jesus who had gone about healing people and preaching powerfully and how he was seen alive after he had been crucified and that his Spirit still lives on in them. I myself became convinced.

Q: How did you become convinced by the claims of Jesus' followers?

A: When they told me the story of how two of them met him on the road to Emmaus, after he had been crucified and buried, you can imagine how skeptical I was. They related how they did not at first recognize him, until he broke the bread, blessed it and gave it to them. Then their eyes were opened and they knew him. And they told of how their hearts had been burning within them as he walked with them and opened the Scriptures to them. I wouldn't have been convinced, but I, too, had the same experience when I joined these followers of Jesus as they broke bread and interpreted the Scriptures. It's true—he lives!

Q: How do you understand God now?

A: In my two books, *The Gospel According to Luke* and *The Acts of the Apostles,* one of the things I tried to show was how the God of the Christians is the same faithful God as the God of the Covenant with Israel and the God of the Hebrew Scriptures. As I see it, God acted dramatically in human history all during the time of the Law and the Prophets. When Jesus was born, a new era began. On the one hand, his coming was a decisive new moment in God's plan. But on the other hand, it is the same faithful God whom Jesus reveals.

Q: Why did you decide to write a Gospel?

A: I was commissioned to write down everything in an orderly fashion by my patron, the excellent Theophilus, whose name means "God-lover." His hope and mine is that through the writing down of this Gospel others may come to know and love God in the person of Jesus.

Q: Where is your home?

A: I live now in Antioch, one of the biggest cities in Asia Minor. There is a sizable Jewish population here and a growing number of Christians. It was here, in fact, that the disciples were first called "Christians" (Acts 11:26).

Q: Are you a medical doctor?

A: There are many who mistakenly think that I am. Actually, it was Irenaeus who started this rumor late in the second century. He thought that I was "Luke, the beloved physician," one of Saint Paul's companions who sent greetings through him to the church at Colossae (Colossians 4:14). The fact is, any educated Greek-speaker knows the medical terminology I use in my books.

Q: Did you travel with Saint Paul?

A: I wish I could say I had known personally the great apostle to the Gentiles. Unfortunately, I never had the pleasure. I've met many who knew him and who have told me all the stories about him. I confess that when I spoke in the first person plural when writing about Saint Paul's journeys in Acts (Chapters 16-28), it was a literary technique I used to make the story more interesting.

Q: What were the sources for your information?

A: I had help from many good sources for my books. Mark had already put in writing his Gospel, which was of great help to me. Although his communities in Rome have different problems and questions than we do, I was able to adapt much of his account to help build up the faith of the Christians in our network of missionary communities. I was also happy to have access to a collection of Jesus' sayings, as well as other oral and written sources about Jesus. I hope I am not being immodest if I tell you that I am not a bad author in my own right. Much of what I wrote I composed myself based on the traditions that came to me.

Placing Our Director in Context

Q: Saint Luke, can you tell us a little about your world?

A: My world has been fairly tranquil, comparatively speaking. In my lifetime Caesar Augustus brought peace, commonly called *pax Augusta*, throughout the Empire. Make no mistake, though, he was a brutal and difficult man. But he did succeed in creating a system of government that maintained a sort of peace throughout our world for centuries to come.

Q: What about Palestine in the time of Jesus?

A: Of course, Jesus was crucified a little more than fifty years before I wrote my Gospel and he lived in Palestine, so his world was different from mine. In Palestine, Caesar set up client kings, like Herod the Great. These kings depended completely on Rome for their power, but they enjoyed considerable freedom in the administration of their kingdoms. Rome reaped many advantages from this system. Of course, if things weren't working, Rome didn't hesitate to step in. By the end of Jesus' life, for example, a Roman-appointed prefect by the name of Pilate was governing Judea. He was under the general supervision of the governor of Syria. The later Roman procurators proved to be insensitive and inept and war against Rome broke out in A.D. 66 in Galilee. It was squelched in A.D. 70 when the Romans razed the Temple in Jerusalem. Palestine was then controlled by a Roman legate. He was directly responsible to the emperor and had the troops of the Tenth Legion at his command. But unrest continued and another revolt broke out in 132, which lasted three years. After that, Jews were expelled from Jerusalem and Christians, too, had scattered to many faraway places.

Q: You seem to be quite a history buff.

A: It's true, I have always been intrigued with history. In fact, I tried in my writings to situate the story of Jesus and the first Christians as clearly as I could in the history of the day. My hope is that you will come to know Jesus as a real person with flesh and blood, who lived in our corner of the world in this particular moment of history.

Q: Did the *pax Augusta* make life better for the ordinary people?

A: The Emperor's peace did not bring well-being to the common people. One of the great problems of our day was that Augustus never really eradicated the poverty and unrest. One thing Augustus tried was a great program of resettlement of people from the lower classes of Italy in new colonies overseas. It helped to alleviate some of the problems in Italy and gave some people a new chance abroad. It also helped spread Latin culture throughout our world. I wish I could say that Augustus's program succeeded in making life liveable for everybody. There was still much inequity between peasants who could barely eke out a living and others who enjoyed sumptuous living. I hope you will be able to see from my writings that the peace Jesus brings has a whole different· quality from the peace the emperor talked about.

Q: What were taxes like?

A: In Palestine of Jesus' day taxes could put you over the brink. With up to one-fourth of your income going for Roman tribute, one-tenth to Herod and one-third to the landowner, you could end up with only one-third of your income left for your replacement fund for next year's seed and for fixing equipment. Plus you had to have some money for social expenditures if there was a wedding or a funeral. There could also come another new little mouth to feed if God so blessed you. God forbid there should be poor rainfall or a pestilence or a famine like the one they had in 25 B.C. under Herod or the one in A.D. 46 under Claudius. Lots of people lost their family farms and had to become tenant farmers, or worse yet, day laborers. Jesus' preaching will make more sense to you if you know this background.

Q: What was the language of the Empire?

A: Although Latin is the official language of the Empire, we all speak Greek as our common language. And people still speak their local languages. Jesus, for instance, spoke Aramaic, as did everyone else in Palestine. But he could get by with enough Greek to do business as a craftsman. And, of course, as a good Jew, he knew Hebrew well enough to read in the synagogue.

Q: Saint Luke, what last words of advice would you like to give us as we begin this retreat?

A: As we begin this retreat together, I invite you to use my writings from your Bible as your primary guide. I originally wrote these accounts for Greek-speaking Gentile Christians in the area of Antioch of Syria in the late eighties. Naturally, our world and the struggles we had then will be very removed from those of your day. Nonetheless, I will try to help you see how God still speaks through this living word to you in a very different time and place from my own. I invite you now to step out in faith on the Word of God.

Day One
Praying Always

Introducing Our Retreat Theme

The theme of our retreat, "Stepping Out on the Word of God," is inspired by a story from Maya Angelou, whom you will remember as the poet who read at the inauguration of President Clinton in 1993. She tells about an early memory of her grandmother, Mamma, "a tall cinnamon-colored woman with a deep, soft voice," who she pictured "standing thousands of feet up in the air on nothing visible." She continues, "That incredible vision was a result of what my imagination would do each time Mamma drew herself up to her full six feet, clasped her hands behind her back, looked up into a distant sky, and said, 'I will step out on the word of God'."

Maya tells of how difficult the Depression was, especially for a single black woman in the South tending her crippled son and two grandchildren. This caused her grandmother frequently to "look up as if she could will herself into the heavens, and tell her family in particular and the world in general, 'I will step out on the word of God. I will step out on the word of God'." She continues, "Immediately I could see her flung into space, moons at her feet and stars at her head, comets swirling around her. Naturally, since Mamma stood out on the word of God, and Mamma was over six feet tall, it wasn't difficult for me to have faith. I grew up knowing that the word of God had power."[1]

I invite you in these seven days to "step out on the Word of God," walking the Way with Jesus, the human face of our faithful God. Begin by telling God your own story, placing whatever burdens you bring in God's gracious care. Ask God to open your eyes in the retelling of the Scriptures to the meaning they hold for your journey. Allow God's love in Jesus to surround you and set your heart on fire. Let God fill you with desire to share that Word to bring hope to others.

Opening Prayer

> Faithful God, you first spoke to Jesus at his baptism,
> where you said, "You are my Son, the Beloved;
> with you I am well pleased" (Luke 3:22).
> It was the constant assurance of your love
> that gave him power for his life and mission.
> Help me to know how beloved I am in your sight
> as I step out on Your Word.
> Give me eyes that are open
> and a heart that burns with desire for you.
>
> Jesus, you walked faithfully in the way of God,
> even when you were uncertain or afraid.
> When you preached and healed,
> you knew God's Word would not fail you.
> When you turned your face to go to Jerusalem,
> you walked with faithful God.
> When you passed through agony and death,
> you clung to the power of God.
> As I follow you, walk with me,
> show me the way.

Holy Spirit, breath of God,
Blow new life upon your Church again.
Give us gifts of prophecy, healing,
inclusive love and courage.
Make us leap for joy
as we step out on the Word of God.

RETREAT SESSION ONE

A retreat is a time to turn more consciously to God in prayer. But the relationship is two-way. It is God who first desires and calls us. In prayer we learn to respond to God's invitation, not only at special retreat times, but in ordinary days as well. The Third Gospel has a special emphasis on prayer. Luke portrays Jesus and others at prayer more times than any other evangelist. But how do we begin to grow into a life of constant prayer?

Joseph Cardinal Bernardin of Chicago, in his final months before succumbing to cancer, wrote of how he had learned to pray always. He recounts that after his ordination he probably prayed as much as any busy young priest. But, he said, "in the mid-1970's, I discovered that I was giving a higher priority to good works than to prayer. I was telling others—seminarians, priests, lay people, and religious—about the importance of prayer, emphasizing that they could not really be connected with the Lord unless they prayed. But I felt somewhat hypocritical in my teaching because I was not setting aside adequate time for personal prayer. It was not that I lacked the desire to pray or that I had suddenly decided prayer was not important. Rather, I was very busy, and I fell into the trap of thinking that my good works were more important than prayer."

He then tells of a dinner with three younger priests at which he asked them to help him with his difficulty in finding time to pray. "Are you sincere in what you request? Do you really want to turn this around?" they asked. He replied, "What could I say? I couldn't say no after what I had just told them!"

"In very direct—even blunt terms—they helped me realize that as a priest and a bishop I was urging a spirituality on others that I was not fully practicing myself. That was a turning point in my life. These priests helped me understand that you have to give what they called 'quality time' to prayer. It can't be done 'on the run.' You have to put aside good time, quality time."[2]

Cardinal Bernardin decided to give God the first hour of his day, no matter what, trying to open the door of his heart even wider to God. He relates how hard it is to let oneself go completely into God's hands. I invite you as you begin this retreat to decide on a particular time each day that will be your "quality time" to step out on the Word of God.

Let us begin with the story of Elizabeth, the first Lucan character whose consistent quality time with God gave her the courage to step out in faith even when God's Word was most puzzling. Allow me to let Elizabeth tell her own story. First pause to read Luke 1:5-25, 39-45, 57-80. How does her story intersect with your own?

Elizabeth: Prayerful Elder

Things had not turned out as we had hoped. Zechariah and I had been married more years than I could count. While we were basically happy, it was always a great sorrow to us that God had not blessed us with children. It was embarrassing as family and friends whispered about us and looked questioningly year after year. I know they were thinking God was punishing us for some terrible sin, but I knew better. It was hard, at first, to hold our heads up. But after so many years, I think people could see that we had both been as faithful as we could to all God's commandments.

Both of us come from priestly families. Zechariah, of course, takes his turn serving in the Temple. It was one time when he was chosen to enter the sanctuary to burn incense that our lives were turned upside down. An angel of God appeared to him right at the altar of incense! Gabriel told him we would have a son and spoke of the marvels God would accomplish through him. You can imagine how disbelieving my poor husband was! Even now it is difficult to reconstruct exactly what happened; he was speechless by the time he came out of the Temple. And for nine months we had to communicate in writing and by gesture.

For my part, it was a shock to ponder the prospect of carrying a child and raising him at my advanced age. I prayed that God would help me understand this strange timing. I needed to withdraw for a while to conserve my strength and to contemplate the meaning of all this. I meditated on our foremothers Sarah, Rebekah, Rachel, Samson's mother, and Hannah, who had all pleaded with God, as I had, to send a child when they had difficulty conceiving.[3] I marveled at the way God accomplished extraordinary things through their sons and prayed that the same would happen with mine. I have always known that God is a God of life and that God does not delight in our suffering. I have persevered faithfully despite my disgrace before others; God has now seen fit to vindicate me.

Even more astonishing was what happened with my relative, Mary. She was in the midst of making wedding plans, when she, too, was visited by Gabriel. You can guess how troubled she was at the sight! But even more distressing was the message he brought: She would conceive a child before she and Joseph came to live together and the child would be called "son of the Most High" and would have an everlasting kingdom. You can imagine her confusion and fear. What would people say when she was found to be with child before she and Joseph began to live together? You can just hear the slander and gossip. It would be a very hard time for her. Although the angel assured her that her son would be called "holy" and that nothing was impossible with God, she still could not understand how all this could happen. Nonetheless, she acceded. Gabriel had told her to come to me for reassurance.

I was so glad when she came to stay with me. By then I was six months along, and it was good to have her there to help me. But if the truth be told, I think I was even more of a help to her. With these grey hairs I could speak convincingly of how God works and I could help her trust God even when it all seemed impossible. We were truly a source of blessing and grace for one another as we spoke of how God was working through us and through the new lives we were birthing.

When it came time for my son to be born, everyone rejoiced with me. But I had to speak up forcefully when it came time for his circumcision and naming. Everyone thought that our only son would surely be named after his father. But Gabriel had been very clear about the name: he was to be called "John," "gift of God." How well his name spoke both of what he meant to us and how he would make known God's grace by his baptizing mission. Only at that moment did Zechariah's voice return. I think it was when he could let go of his doubts and questions and abandon himself to God's faithfulness at this marvelous moment, that God loosened his tongue again. For my part, I still do not understand God's ways, but I sit quietly in prayer with God as much as I can each day. That is what gave me the strength to make it through all the difficult things God has asked of me. And in my golden years, I think God can't help but take delight in me and all we have been through together. I have a great peaceful sense that God walks with me always.

Let me introduce you now to Mary, and let her tell you more of her story. Pause to read Luke 1:26-38, 46-56; 2:1-52. How is God speaking to you through her story?

Mary: The Compassion of God

Elizabeth has already told you how my story began. Let me resume with the birth of my son. As you know, I was very young and much less experienced in the ways of God than my elder kinswoman. I thank God for the support she gave me in those difficult months as I tried to understand what was happening to me. Elizabeth was always so sure that God was bringing blessing and goodness out of what seemed like a horrendous situation. How could I help but trust her wisdom? She was such a model of constant prayer; she seemed to know God so intimately. She was a wonderful guide, reminding me of how God had used the wombs of women so often in our past to bring salvation to our people. As I struggled to see God in all that transpired, my troubledness gave way to joy at being the next in a long line of Israelite women to give birth to the very compassion of God! I continued guarding everything in my heart, pondering what it all would mean.

After Jesus was born, Joseph and I were eager to take him to the Temple, as the Law prescribed. I will never forget two of the people we met there because of the extraordinary things they said to us. The first was an old man named Simeon. You could tell how close he was to

God; he was very devout and filled with the Spirit. He took our child in his arms and blessed God and spoke of how he could now die in peace because he had beheld the salvation of God. I was disturbed, though, by his next words. He looked at me when he said, "This child is destined for the falling and the rising of many in Israel, and to be a sign that will be opposed so that the inner thoughts of many will be revealed—and a sword will pierce your own soul too" (Luke 2:34-35). It reminded me of the sword of discrimination that the prophet Ezekiel (14:17) talked of that would divide the faithful from the unfaithful. If Simeon was trying to tell me that I would have to struggle like anyone else to understand my son and what God had in store for him, he was surely right!

There was also an old woman prophet named Anna. They say she had been a perfect wife the seven years she lived with her husband before he died. After that, no one remembered a time that they didn't see her worshiping in the Temple, day and night, fasting and praying. Local people say she's now about 105 years old—just like Judith our foremother (Judith 8:6). When she saw us approach, her eyes lit up and she gave loud thanks to God. She, too, said she had been waiting a long time for the redemption of Jerusalem. And she started talking about Jesus to anyone who would listen.

I tucked all these things away in my memory and I keep reflecting back on them whenever I pray, which is almost always. I can see, the older I get, how constant God's love has been for us. The same faithful God who walked with our ancestors has now shown utmost compassion to me in all that has happened since my son was born. I did not always understand what God was doing, but I was given the grace to continue to step out on the Word of God in trust. I think I raised my son well. I tried to teach him to turn to God at every moment. I told him how I knew from the moment he was conceived that God's Spirit was with him in a special way and that God would never abandon him. I hope that you, too, have known God's strength and comfort in this way in your life. God continues to be born in every person's life. How has that happened for you? How do you help others to recognize God's birth in their lives?

I invite you now to listen to my son as he tells you how he learned to step out on the Word of God. Let your own experience of God be mirrored in his.

Jesus: Prophet Steeped in Prayer

I was young and ambitious—I had my whole life and career ahead of me. Joseph had taught me all about working with wood and stone and I was becoming quite expert after years of helping him on the job. We were luckier than many; with a trade and a little plot of land we were fairly secure economically. I was almost thirty years old and my family had been talking to me about marriage and beginning a family of my own.

But there was something nagging at me. I had learned from my mother from the time I was very young how to immerse myself in prayer. I sensed that God had something important in store for me. At Passover time we made a pilgrimage to Jerusalem for the feast. I heard that my cousin John had taken on a very ascetical life-style and was preaching out in the desert. I was drawn to him to see if my answer could be found there. I was praying while people were coming to be baptized and I asked John to baptize me, too. It was then that I heard God's answer. I felt the Spirit rush upon me and I heard God's voice clearly telling me how beloved I am and how pleased God is with me. This was an experience I will never forget. I had always been surrounded by a sense of God's presence and love. But in this particular moment I experienced it in a way that would never leave me. I knew from that moment that whatever God asked, I could do, by stepping out on that Word of God's love.

After that I started preaching and healing people and I began to gather a few disciples. But I never skimped on my time for prayer. I searched out deserted spots to be alone with God, communing with the One who had so gifted me. Sometimes I would go alone; sometimes I would take some of my followers. One memorable incident was a time when Peter, John and James went with me up a mountain to pray. I had been troubled about whether to stay in Galilee, where so much good was being accomplished. But if I was to make a further impact I would have to take my prophetic message to the seat of religious power of my people. But I was no fool, either. I knew that Jerusalem always kills the prophets. Deep in contemplation, I got my answer—and the others told me later they could see it by the way my face lit up! My death would not be the end of everything. The Law and the Prophets pointed toward a new "exodus"—a new liberation of God's people that would come precisely through my death.[4] It was then that I knew clearly that I must set my face to go to Jerusalem.

These foundational experiences of God's love directed the whole course of my life. Pause now to reflect on your own experience of God. When have you heard God's voice telling you how beloved you are? Let it echo in your heart once again. Savor this love and let it surround every part of you. What dramatic turning points have you had in your life? Have you known God's guidance in difficult decisions? Reflect on how God has always been with you and how God buoys you up in the critical moments.

While God always begins the love affair with us, God waits eagerly for our response. But what are we to say? How are we to address God? How can we express our thanks? How do we ask for what we need? These are questions my first disciples also put to me. I gave them a few simple pointers:

> "When you pray, say: Father, hallowed be your name. Your kingdom come. Give us each day our daily bread. And forgive us our sins, for we ourselves forgive everyone indebted to us. And do not bring us to the time of trial" (Luke 11:2-4).

As other Jews before me had done, I suggested to my disciples that at times they should call God "Father,"[5] particularly when they were seeking refuge from affliction or looking for assurance of forgiveness. In our world the Roman emperor claimed the title *pater patriae* and ruled the empire as the head of a patriarchal family. I wanted my followers to pray a little subversively. By invoking God as our only "Father" we claim God's power over every other kind of power.[6] Praying this way was tantamount to saying that God, not the emperor, is the supreme power!

This was only one of many ways in which I taught my disciples to speak with God. No one image can ever fully express the mystery of God and what God's reign is like. I used so many images and stories about God to try to give my disciples words to speak with God about whatever was their present experience. Were they finding delight in the fruitful work of the ministry God had given them to do? Then imagine God as a woman baking bread, providing fulfilling fare for all her family. Were they discouraged about trying to bring back the lost who were difficult to find? Then picture God as a shepherd who searches everywhere for a lost sheep. Or like a woman who expends every ounce of energy to unearth a stray coin and then throws a lavish party to celebrate the finding of the lost one. What experience do you now want to speak about with God? What image of God encompasses that experience?

One other important time to turn to God in prayer is in moments of crisis. I wanted to help my disciples move beyond frantic pleas of rescue to a deeper level of trust and assurance of God's presence whenever they were being asked to endure what might seem impossible. For me, the last night with my followers was just such a moment. We had celebrated together the Passover supper and afterward we went out to the Mount of Olives. The eeriness of passing by the tombs in the Kidron Valley with the full moon was unnerving, and I began to realize that this was probably the night the authorities would come for me.

As we reached Gethsemane I prayed with all my strength that there might be some other way. I asked God if it was possible for this cup to pass me by. I looked over at my disciples and tried to focus on how powerfully God had worked through us. I tried to gain strength from knowing that they would be capable to carry on after I was dead. But they had succumbed to the wine and lateness of the hour. They were fast asleep.

Again and again I tried to pray as I had learned: not my will, but yours. And as my mother taught me: Nothing is impossible with God. But what was God's will? Should I escape over the Mount of Olives into the Judean desert? They would never find me there. Perhaps after a time of hiding I could quietly continue my ministry of healing and teaching. No, I had no sense of peace about such a choice. And then it was as if God sent an angel to strengthen me. There would be no changing the course I had set upon, but I knew God was with me. The prayer steeled me as I took this one last great step out on the Word of God.

How has a life of learning to pray always helped you

in moments of crisis? How has God been present to you
in such times?

For Reflection

- *Decide on a time each day in which you can give "quality
  time" to God in prayer, even if it is only fifteen minutes.*

- *Develop a way in which you can continually turn to God
  in prayer. Choose a mantra, that is, a favorite phrase like "I
  will step out on the Word of God" or "Jesus, mercy" or
  "Spirit of God, breathe in me" that can quickly put you in
  mind that you walk always with God.*

- *How is God speaking to you in the stories of Elizabeth,
  Mary and Jesus at prayer?*

- *Name a particular grace you have received in prayer and
  give thanks to God for this gift. In what way is God asking
  you to share the fruits of your contemplation with others?*

Closing Prayer

Jesus, you taught your disciples,
"Ask, and it will be given you;
search, and you will find;
knock, and the door will be opened for you"
   (Luke 11:9).
Teach us now to seek you at all times
and to receive graciously the gifts you want to give.

You assure us that just as parents
give good gifts to their children,
so our God gives the Spirit to those who ask.
Give us your Spirit who helps us in our weakness.

When we do not know how to pray as we ought,
let your Spirit intercede
with sighs too deep for words.

Give us hearts on fire and eyes that see
that we may share your love with others.
Give us courage, we pray,
to step out on your Word.

Notes

[1] Maya Angelou, *Wouldn't Take Nothing for my Journey Now* (New York: Random House, 1993), pp. 73-74.

[2] Joseph Cardinal Bernardin, *The Gift of Peace* (Chicago: Loyola Press, 1997), pp. 4-6.

[3] Sarah: Genesis 16; Rebekah: Genesis 25; Rachel: Genesis 30; Samson's mother: Judges 13; Hannah: 1 Samuel 1-2.

[4] See Barbara E. Reid, *The Transfiguration: A Source—and Redaction— Critical Study of Luke 9:28-36. Cahiers de la Revue Biblique* 32. Paris: Gabalda, 1993; and "Voices and Angels: What Were They Talking about at the Transfiguration? A Redaction-critical Study of Luke 9:28-36," *Biblical Research* 34 (1989), pp. 19-31.

[5] See, e.g., Sirach 23:1,4; Wisdom 2:16-20; 14:3; 3 Maccabees 6:3-4,7-8; Tobit 13:4; 4Q372 1.16; 4Q460; fragment 2 of the *Apocalypse of Ezekiel;* Josephus *Antiquities* 2.6.8 152; Philo, *Op. mund.* 10, 21, pp. 72-75; *m. Yoma* 8:9; *b. Ta`an.* 25b. See Mary Rose D'Angelo, "*ABBA* and 'Father': Imperial Theology and the Jesus Traditions," *Journal of Biblical Literature* 111/4 (1992), pp. 611-630; James Charlesworth, "A Caveat on Textual Transmission and the Meaning of *Abba*: A Study of the Lord's Prayer" in *The Lord's Prayer and Other Texts from the Greco-Roman Era*, J. H. Charlesworth, ed. (Valley Forge, Penn.: Trinity Press International, 1994), pp. 1-14.

[6] The notion that "Abba" was a kind of baby talk, like "Daddy" and expressed a special kind of tenderness between Jesus and God has been shown to be mistaken by James Barr in "*Abba* Isn't Daddy," *Journal of Theological Studies* ns 39 (1988), pp. 28-47, and "*Abba* and the Familiarity of Jesus' Speech," *Theology* 91 (1988), pp. 173-179.

DAY TWO
Accepting Costly Love

Coming Together in the Spirit

> "There is always something left to love. And if you
> ain't learned that, you ain't learned nothing. Have
> you cried for that boy today? I don't mean for
> yourself and for the family 'cause we lost the money.
> I mean for him: what he been through and what it
> done to him. Child, when do you think is the time to
> love somebody the most? When they done good and
> made things easy for everybody? Well, then, you
> ain't through learning—because that ain't the time at
> all. It's when he's at his lowest and can't believe in
> hisself 'cause the world done whipped him so!
> When you starts measuring somebody, measure him
> right, child, measure him right. Make sure you done
> taken into account what hills and valleys he come
> through before he got to wherever he is."[1]

This dialogue from *A Raisin in the Sun* captures well what
the parables in Luke 15 are trying to say. Take time now
to read these three parables: the shepherd searching for a
wayward sheep (15:3-7), the woman seeking a lost coin
(15:8-10) and a father taking costly actions to gain back
his sons (15:11-32).

Defining Our Thematic Context

Stepping out on the Word of God, the theme of our retreat, entails taking many distinct steps. Each step is part of our larger journey and builds on the one before. On Day One we walked with Elizabeth and Zechariah, Mary, Jesus, Simeon and Anna. From them we learned how to step out on the Word of God in continual prayer. As we begin Day Two we walk with one who has stepped out on his own, but has ended on the wrong path, destitute, and seemingly unlovable. His story invites us to open our hearts to accept God's costly love, wherever we find ourselves on the journey.

Opening Prayer

Pardon is your name,
Forgiveness your eternal title,
by "Mercy as vast as the universe" are you known.
Grant me, O Gracious One,
your great gift of pardon.

I have searched for it
in every pocket and hiding place;
I cannot find it, your gift of Self.
I know it is here,
buried beneath my pain,
somewhere in a back corner of my heart:
but for now it is lost.

Make me your messenger
of the good news I cannot now speak.
Give to me words of forgiveness,
the healing touch of pardon,
the love that weds two as one.

I know that to forgive is divine,
but I am no deity,
and I fear I will be a demon,
who, by failing to forgive,
will spread the kingdom of darkness.

Remind me ten times and more
of all that you have forgiven me—
without even waiting for my sorrow,
the very instant that I slipped and sinned.
Remind me ten thousand times and more
of your endless absolution,
not even sorrow required on my part,
so broad the bounty of your love.

Yes, I can—I will—forgive
as you have forgiven me.[2]

RETREAT SESSION TWO

At the beginning of a retreat we often start with self-examination. Often it is the first chance we have to pause from the intense business of our everyday concerns. Left alone and in silence with ourselves, our faults and failings loom large. This, is, however, precisely the wrong starting point. One thing that becomes clear from Luke's Gospel is that it is God who starts us out on our journey with an immense act of love. And no matter how far off the course we wander, God will always draw us back with great loving arms. The good news is that it is not up to us to get ourselves back. This is such a hard thing to grasp, that Jesus told it in story form a number of different times. Luke tells three parables, all with the same point. Pause now to read Luke 15:1-32. Imagine with me that

Luke is telling us his understanding of these stories in his own voice.

A Wayward Sheep (Luke 15:1-7)

As I understand it, Jesus once told this story to a group of Pharisees and scribes who were criticizing him for eating with outcasts. I think he was trying to say that he himself acts like the shepherd in the story because that is what God does. It's easy to see the point when you put it into story form.

A shepherd who is in charge of one hundred sheep will most certainly take great care not to lose one. Most probably a herd that size belongs to several members of his clan. Or, if they all belong to one person, the owner himself is rich enough to hire the shepherd to do the dirty work of herding. In either case, the shepherd is answerable to others if any sheep disappears. If, God forbid, a sheep should be attacked and killed, the shepherd had better produce the carcass to prove that he did not take it for himself.

So, having lost one of them, he will certainly leave the other ninety-nine in the care of another and go to search out the stray. In the craggy hillsides of Palestine, this is no easy task. And though the sheep may hear the shepherd call, if it has become frightened it will not be able to get up and go to the shepherd. All it may do is bleat so the master can retrieve it. By the time the shepherd finds it, the poor sheep is in such a state of collapse that the shepherd has to pick it up and carry it back on his shoulders. Imagine lugging a seventy-pound sheep over rocks and hills!

There is a marvelous statue in the Rockefeller Museum in Jerusalem of a third-century depiction of Jesus as the Good Shepherd that beautifully captures this scene. In it the sheep is twice the size of the shepherd, yet the shepherd is smiling from ear to ear in delight at finding the stray. What an image of the great cost God is willing to pay to get back the lost one! It is striking that it is God, the shepherd, who brings the stray back. The lost ones cannot make it back by their own efforts.[3]

Finally, the shepherd's joy spills over to all his friends and neighbors in great festivity. I remember the apostle Paul observed that "If one member suffers, all suffer together with it; if one member is honored, all rejoice together with it"(1 Corinthians 12:26). So, too, the losing and finding of the sheep is a communal affair, just as is the reconciliation of any of us to God.

I found this story disturbing. On the one hand, a picture of God who was so willing to expend costly love, unearned, to bring back one who was straying is an immense relief. If I am the one in trouble, all I have to do is be willing to accept that great love and let myself be embraced by those tender arms. It lifts a huge burden if it is not up to me to put things right. On the other hand, I am used to being in control. I look to myself and ask, "What do I have to do to make it right again?"

Perhaps the Pharisees and scribes to whom Jesus first told this parable, were not so comfortable with it either. One thing I want to set straight is that these were basically good religious people. Readers of my Gospel often think of the Pharisees as hypocritical, rigid and legalistic. And that is the impression I give. Actually, I was not trying to tell you how they really were historically. Rather, I used them as a foil to Jesus. I always made their understanding of God's reign opposite that of Jesus. As you read of their increasingly hostile response to Jesus in the Gospel, I wanted to provoke the opposite response in you.

Nonetheless, I think that when Jesus asked these religious leaders to put themselves in the shoes of a shepherd it was rather shocking to them. Good Jews of Jesus' day tended to look down on shepherds. They were thought to be dishonest and thieving. Some of them would lead their herds onto other peoples' land to graze. Once in a while they would try to pilfer the produce of the flock.[4] And of course, they weren't too pleasant to be around, unless you liked the smell of sheep!

On the other hand, there was a very clever twist to Jesus' story of the shepherd. Every good Jew knew well Psalm 23, which begins, "The Lord is my shepherd, I shall not want." And everybody would remember that many of Israel's great leaders, like Moses and David, were shepherds. And people would remember Ezekiel's biting critique of Israel's "shepherds," that is, religious leaders, who were looking out for their own well-being instead of that of their flock (Ezekiel 34:1-16).

Jesus was trying to get the Pharisees and scribes to see that they, in order to be good shepherds of God's flock, needed first to be able to accept the kind of costly love God offers them. Once they were able to walk in the light of that love, then they, like Jesus, could in turn offer that love to others who were lost and in need of being found. If they had a hard time with this story, I can imagine how they reacted to another version Jesus told.

A Lost Coin (Luke 15:8-10)

This parable tells the same story, but from the world of women.[5] It describes the same diligent searching to find something precious that is lost and the same rejoicing when it is found. This point is sometimes missed. Some who have heard this story think of the woman as miserly or careless. Some imagine that she is being petty, looking for a lost penny of her extra spending money. In fact both these parables come from the everyday world of poor people who work very hard just to survive. The woman is searching for the coin because she needs it to feed her family.

One other false impression that some people have about this parable comes from their having seen modern day Bedouin women who have beautiful headdresses adorned with coins. They then imagine that the woman in Jesus' story has lost one of the decorative pieces of her headdress or necklace. The whole piece of jewelry loses its value if one coin is missing. As interesting as this suggestion is, it cannot be what Jesus intended because Jewish women of the first century did not wear such headdresses; they belong to modern Bedouin women. In reality the coin is as precious to the woman as the sheep is to the shepherd and as children are to parents.

Like the shepherd, the woman expends great effort to recover the lost coin. Houses in Palestine were cramped, with small windows that allowed for only a little ventilation, and not much light. The floors were of packed dirt or cobblestones—affording nooks where a coin could easily be lost forever. The woman uses up expensive oil to light a lamp and she expends much energy sweeping and searching in all the cracks and corners. And like the shepherd who finds his precious sheep, the woman invites all her friends to celebrate with her when her costly efforts succeed.

If Jesus' original audience of scribes and Pharisees rankled at the image of God as a despised shepherd, you can imagine how they reacted to this version, posing God as a woman. In a patriarchal world such an image is very difficult to grasp. Yet Jesus was well within his Jewish tradition in setting forth such a notion. Here is how I imagine he might explain it to you:

I have always been puzzled by the resistance I've encountered in good religious people to think of God in feminine images. Maybe it is not so hard for me because my own mother taught me to think of God in so many diverse ways. And she herself embodied everything that I imagine God to be. She introduced me to the places in our Scriptures where God is portrayed as a mother giving birth (like Deuteronomy 32:18 and Isaiah 42:14). And there is Isaiah speaking of God's tenderness as that of a mother consoling her child (Isaiah 49:15; 66:13). I think, too, of the way the Psalmist talks of God's care for us like that of a mother eagle for her brood (Psalm 91:4). I found this an apt image to express my own care for Jerusalem (Luke 13:34).

Perhaps it was my sensitivity to this reality that both genders embody godliness that made my preaching attractive to women followers as well as men. We could never have managed to reach all the people we did in our healing and preaching ministry if it weren't for the women. Some of them financed the mission (Luke 8:3), and they were also powerful preachers and teachers. It was they who stood by me to the end and who were the first to find the tomb empty. But more of that later.

If you have not yet had an opportunity to pray with God as she is revealed in female forms, perhaps this retreat is a good moment to enter this new realm. Choose one of the images from the Hebrew Scriptures that I have mentioned above and enter into this more deeply. As you pray with this text, ask God to open to you new ways of experiencing the divine in both female and male incarnations. Recall that every way we picture God falls short of the reality of who God truly is. Yet God has been revealed to us in human flesh. Recall that Genesis 1:27 assures us that both men and women reveal the image of God. Invite God to help you be

able to accept being found by God in such
surprising forms as a woman searching for a coin or
as a despised shepherd.

The final story in the triad makes the same point. This
time the setting is a conflictive family situation—perhaps
even what we would call today a dysfunctional family.[6]

Two Alienated Sons (Luke 15:11-32)

This is not an easy story. When you know what Jesus'
world was like, there are all kinds of things that are
"wrong with this picture." There are three characters and
three different perspectives on accepting costly love. At
the outset all three are present as a difficult drama begins.
It starts with the younger son making an outrageous
request for his share of the estate. It was as if he had said
to his father, "I wish you were dead"—a highly shameful
thing in this culture. What is all the more shocking is that
the father gives it to him and that the older son does
nothing to intervene or to help reconcile. We also wonder
where the mother is; she could play a conciliatory role.
What kind of family is this?

As might typically happen when a country boy goes
off to the big city, he soon wastes all his money and is in
dire need. He attaches himself to a patron, but his
situation is no better. Finally, he "came to himself," that is,
he remembers who he is and realizes that he cannot go on
this way. Knowing he cannot return home as a son, he
remembers his father's hired hands and how well paid
they are. He concocts a plan to be able to fill his belly by
working for his father. Though the words he rehearses to
say to his father sound like he is repenting, "Father, I
have sinned against heaven and before you; I am no
longer worthy to be called your son; treat me like one of
your hired hands" (15:18-19), in fact they echo those of

Pharaoh to Moses, "I have sinned against the LORD your God, and against you" (Exodus 10:16). Like Pharaoh, who just wants Moses to call off the plagues, the young son is simply looking for a way to survive.

What happens next in the story strains credibility. A father in this situation would have rent his garments and declared this boy no longer his son once he departed with the family inheritance. Not only the father, but the whole family, clan and village, would have turned in horror at the loss of their precious land and goods to foreigners. Was it the mother who chipped away at the father's wounded honor, pleading with him to accept their boy back should he return? That part of the story was never filled in for me.

But I couldn't make up such an ending as I heard to this parable. The father watched and waited for that boy, and when he first caught sight of him, far off, he ran to him (no dignified patriarch runs in this culture!) and he regaled him with all the trappings of a free man: a fine robe, a ring and sandals. He wouldn't let the boy finish his prepared speech; the youngster never got to propose how he would try to earn his way. The father just took upon himself all the hurt and shame. He paid a great price to get back this son, and the boy had no will left to refuse this boundless love. The father embraced the boy tightly to shield him from any abuse that might be directed to such a disloyal child. And together they returned home.

Then the father gave a great feast, trying to give back to the community in reparation for the harm done by his son. Incredibly, all the neighbors accepted the invitation and the father regained his lost honor with them. It might have been a happy ending at this point, had Jesus left out the older brother. But his part in the story probably strikes home more closely with all those who try to do the right thing throughout their lives and seem to get nothing for it.

That older son was just as alienated as his younger brother. He should have been helping to host the celebration, when instead his father has to plead with him to come in to the party. Such a scene is really unimaginable. Fathers command and sons obey. No father pleads with his son to fulfill his filial obligations.

What is tragic is that the older son thinks of himself as a slave to his father. He is not so different from his younger brother who wants to be a hired servant. He, too, thinks he can earn his share of his father's estate. The father urges him to see that all he has is already offered to both his sons, if they are prepared to accept this love for which the father has paid so dearly. It is a love that also has the power to heal the broken relationship between the two brothers (notice that he refers to "that son of yours" rather than "my brother"). The story of the older son remains unfinished. Does he go into the party? Does he accept the love offered to him? Can he rejoice in the reconciliation with his lost brother? Or will he remain lost himself in his slavishness and joyless resentment?

This parable of Jesus is one more way of repeating the theme of the shepherd searching for the sheep and the woman looking her coin. Like them, the father pays a great price to get back his lost sons. The father offers a model of how to pastor well. After taking upon himself shame and the consequences of disrupted relationships, he watches for the opportune moment to bring back the lost one. His first concern is for the one that is lost, not for his own well-being.

From the perspective of the sons, there are two ways of being lost. The story of the younger son can offer a hopeful way out for anyone who feels like they have hit rock bottom. That of the older son is aimed at good people who try to do what is right, but don't always see their own need for what the father has to offer. Neither one can make it back into right relation with parents and siblings on his own. It is the father who brings them back. We know that the first son accepts the invitation. Does the second?

For Reflection

- *Ask God to give you the grace to accept the free and costly love that God is offering to you. Abandon yourself into this loving embrace of God. Let go of trying to put things right by yourself. Let yourself feel wrapped in a parent's strong arms, carried on a shepherd's shoulders, restored by a diligent woman. Enjoy the rejoicing and celebrating at your being found.*

- *Dwell with the image of God as a woman who relentlessly seeks the well-being of creation. What is revealed as you enter further into the mystery of God who is beyond male and female, yet reflected in both?*

- *As you experience receiving these gifts, what response is God asking?*

Closing Prayer

Amazing Grace! How sweet the sound
That saved [and set me free]!
I once was lost, but now am found,
Was blind, but now I see.

'Twas grace that taught my heart to fear,
And grace my fears relieved;
How precious did that grace appear

The hour I first believed!

Through many dangers, toils and snares
I have already come;
'Tis grace has brought me safe thus far,
And grace will lead me home.

God, you have promised good to me,
Your word my hope secures;
You will my shield and portion be
As long as life endures.

When we've been there ten thousand years,
Bright shining as the sun,
We've no less days to sing God's praise
Than when we first begun.[7]

Notes

[1] Lorraine Hansberry, *A Raisin in the Sun* (New York: The New American Library, 1959), p. 121.

[2] "A Psalm of Pardon" by Edward Hays, in *Prayers for a Planetary Pilgrim* (Easton, Kan.: Forest of Peace Books, 1988), p. 175.

[3] See further Kenneth E. Bailey, *Finding the Lost: Cultural Keys to Luke 15*, Concordia Scholarship Today (St. Louis: Concordia, 1992); *Poet and Peasant* and *Through Peasant Eyes*, 2 vols. in 1. (Grand Rapids, Mich.: Eerdmans, 1976, 1980), pp. 158-206.

[4] Joachim Jeremias, *Jerusalem in the Time of Jesus* (Philadelphia: Fortress, 1969) 303-305, 310, cites examples from the Mishnah that list herdsmen among the despised trades.

[5] See further Barbara E. Reid, *Choosing the Better Part? Women in the Gospel of Luke* (Collegeville, Minn.: The Liturgical Press, 1996), pp. 179-189.

[6] See Richard Rohrbaugh, "A Dysfunctional Family and its Neighbors (Luke 15:11b-132)," in *Jesus and His Parables*. Ed. V.G. Shillington (Edinburgh: T.&T. Clark, 1997), pp. 141-164.

[7] Text stanzas 1-4: John Newton 1725-1807 (with adaptations of inclusive language to v. 4 and personal adaptations to v. 1); stanza 5 ascribed to John Rees, 1859.

Day Three
Giving All / Keeping Some

Coming Together in the Spirit

It happened in August, 1990. I had arrived in Tel Aviv
with a group that I would guide on an eleven-week study
program in the Holy Land. I was tired from the travel, but
excited to be in Israel again. We each grabbed a luggage
cart and waited for our bags to tumble down onto the
conveyor. As each one claimed a suitcase I looked
anxiously for mine. And I waited...and waited...and
waited. And then the conveyor shut down and there were
no more bags! In the pit of my stomach I had an awful,
panicky feeling. What if they've lost my bags forever?

True to Jesus' instructions to his disciples on their first
mission, I had not packed a walking staff—it wouldn't fit!
Nor had I taken any food; I trusted they would feed us on
the plane. But I certainly had packed many changes of
clothing, and my walking shoes, and my backpack, and
all my notes and maps and books—all my things were
lost somewhere in the bowels of airline baggage
handling! I was suddenly at the mercy of others for every
mundane need. I didn't even have a toothbrush. In some
ways, it was a very small taste of leaving everything
behind to go on mission for Jesus—even if the stripping
of all my possessions was involuntary!

Defining Our Thematic Context

I invited you on Day One to step out on the Word of God in constant prayer. Recall now the mantra you chose to help you become aware of God's constant loving presence and God's desire to be with you. Ask Jesus to help you pray always as he did. Yesterday, in reflecting on the lost and found sheep, coin and sons, we discovered how God is the one who does the hard work of bringing us back into the divine loving embrace when we become lost. I invited you to meditate on the startling ways in which God is revealed as female and male, as poor and marginalized. As we continue to let ourselves be found by God, listen today to what response God asks of you in your particular economic circumstances. What will allow you to step out more freely on the Word of God?

Opening Prayer

Take, Lord, receive
all my liberty
my memory, understanding,
my entire will.

Give me only your love
and your grace:
that's enough for me.
Your love and your grace
are enough for me.

Take, Lord, receive
all I have and possess.
You have given all to me;
now I return it.

Take, Lord, receive,

all is yours now;
dispose of it
wholly according to your will.[1]

Retreat Session Three

I, Luke, assure you there is no one-size-fits-all when it comes to discipleship. When I first heard about the "Way" I expected that the more experienced disciples would outline for me the precise things I needed to do to be a good follower of Jesus. To my surprise, they told me a number of stories of the calling of the first followers but their responses varied—and none was thought better than another! Let me tell you about some of the more memorable ones: Simon, James and John (Luke 5:1-11); Levi (5:27-32); Mary Magdalene, Joanna and Susanna (8:1-3); Zacchaeus (19:1-10); and a poor widow (21:1-4). I will let each of them tell you their own stories. I invite you to walk in each of their shoes and let God speak to you through their experiences. What response is God asking of you? Pause now to read the story of the call of the first disciples in Luke 5:1-11. Join me in listening to the way Simon experienced it. How does your call as a disciple intersect with his story?

Simon: The Skeptical Fisherman

My name is Simon, although now I mostly go by Peter. Let me tell you how it all started. It was a day pretty much like any other. We'd been fishing all night, but we did not have much to show for it. That happens sometimes. James and John tend to worry a little more on days like this, but our business is holding its own. We have our steady customers, and God has blessed us with enough profit to make ends meet for our families and then some. It's the taxes that give us the biggest headaches, but we work hard and trust God will provide.

We hadn't expected that our lives would be changed so completely after that day. A new preacher from Nazareth, Jesus, had come to our village. He was related to John, whom they called the Baptizer. Jesus provoked mixed reactions in his own hometown, but here in Capernaum many were taken with him. He claimed to have the Spirit of God upon him and spoke eloquently. He healed a number of people, including my mother-in-law. She had been sick with a very high fever. We asked Jesus if he could do anything for her—what harm is there in asking?—and she was immediately better after he stood over her and rebuked the fever. It was good to have her up and around again. It was a strain on my wife to have sole care of the household while her mother was ill. We offered Jesus hospitality, in our typical fashion. I thought that things would get back to normal after that, but by nightfall all sorts of people who were sick and possessed by demons flocked to our house to be cured by him. And every one of them left healed!

I was mulling over all this while we were fishing that night. Then there he was at the shore in the morning while we were washing our nets. And the crowds were still following him. He got into my boat and asked me to put out a little way from the shore so he could teach from the boat. As I said, it had been a slow night, so there wasn't much work to do that morning. I figured I could spare a bit of my time. After all, he had helped me out with my mother-in-law.

I thought he was a little crazy, though, when he finished speaking and asked me to put out into the deep water and lower the nets for a catch. You could tell he didn't know anything about fishing. I pointed out to him that we had been hard at it all night but caught nothing, but then I decided to humor him. Did I have the surprise of my life! The nets filled up with so many fish I thought they were going to break. I yelled to James and John to bring the other boat and both boats were almost swamped with the weight of the catch. With that, I was really afraid. What manner of man was this? I blurted out that he better get away from me because I'm just an ordinary sinner. Clearly, he was a man of God and I had gotten close enough to know I didn't belong with the likes of him.

I'll never forget what he said next, "Do not be afraid. From now on you will be catching people." I wondered what in the world he meant. How do you catch people? All my life I've been catching fish. I realized he was asking me to let go of my fishing business and all that was familiar to start a new venture with him. But I felt so unworthy in the presence of one who could fill my net to the breaking point when I myself had caught nothing. Moreover, if I joined him, how would I feed my family? How would my relatives and friends react? I'm no preacher or healer. What would he have me do? And then, all of a sudden, I found myself wanting to step out on his word, in blind faith, and follow him. What gave me further courage was that James and John were ready to do the same! Thank God you never have to step out all alone! I realized that together we could do whatever Jesus was asking of us. So we left everything.

Little did we know then what was in store for us. The next thing we knew, he was asking us to go out to preach the reign of God and to heal people! As if that weren't daunting enough he then gave us very explicit instructions: "Take nothing for your journey, no staff, nor bag, nor bread, nor money—not even an extra tunic.

Whatever house you enter, stay there, and leave from
there. Wherever they do not welcome you, as you are
leaving that town shake the dust off your feet as a
testimony against them" (9:3-5). That time I really did
think he was crazy. I almost left him. I could understand
it if he wanted us to go lightly so we wouldn't be
encumbered by too much baggage. But he actually told us
to take *nothing*! No staff to fend off wild animals or
robbers; no bag to carry anything at all; nothing to eat; no
money to buy necessities at our destination; and not even
a change of clothing. He was sending us out completely
defenseless and vulnerable, making us totally dependent
on our hosts. Not only that he told us not to go looking
around for the best accommodations, but to stay in
whatever place first welcomed us. And we should be
prepared for some who would slam the door in our face.

At first I thought this was some kind of joke. First
Jesus said he was giving us power to heal and preach, but
then he asked us to go out under the guise of complete
powerlessness! Power, as I knew it, came from physical
strength, brute force, economic security, job and family
stability. I couldn't fathom who in the world would listen
to so-called "good news" from a starving beggar! What
kind of persuasive power could be found in that?

It would take many years for me to understand and
live out of that power in vulnerability that he taught us.
Only after his crucifixion and resurrection did we fully
grasp that our mission was not about possessing the
fullness of truth and then passing it on. Rather, we came
to see that it is in the give-and-take of immersing
ourselves in the lives of the people to whom we are sent,
of letting go, not only of our possessions, but of our very
selves as we serve others that God, who is so vulnerable
as to take on human form, is revealed!

You know, I didn't go looking for this, and it hasn't

always been easy, but as I reflect back, I have no regrets at all. This business of leaving everything isn't for everybody. I remember one time when a rich ruler asked Jesus what he had to do to inherit eternal life (Luke 18:18-30). When Jesus told him to keep the commandments, he said he always had, but he was still looking for something else. So Jesus invited him to sell everything and give it to the poor and then follow him. The poor man went away sad—he was very rich and just couldn't do it. It was then that Jesus assured us that those of us who had left family and homes for the sake of the reign of God would receive very much more both in this life and in the next. He's right. What more could anyone ask? I'm as contented as another fisherman in a story I've since heard:

> The rich industrialist from the North was horrified to find the Southern fisherman lying lazily beside his boat, smoking a pipe.
>
> "Why aren't you out fishing?" said the industrialist.
>
> "Because I have caught enough fish for the day," said the fisherman.
>
> "Why don't you catch some more?"
>
> "What would I do with it?"
>
> "You could earn more money," was the reply. "With that you could have a motor fixed to your boat and go into deeper waters and catch more fish. Then you would make enough to buy nylon nets. These would bring you more fish and more money. Soon you would have enough money to own two boats...maybe even a fleet of boats. Then you would be a rich man like me."
>
> "What would I do then?"
>
> "Then you could really enjoy life."
>
> "What do you think I am doing right now?"[2]

Where does your contentment lie? Is there a new

invitation to you to let go of something that binds you as you step out on the Word of God?

Mary of Magdala: Supportive Disciple

Not everyone who was called to be a disciple was asked to leave everything behind. There are drastic changes in store for anyone who follows Jesus. But what disciples do with their possessions depends on the ministry to which they are called. Another example is that of the Galilean women. Pause now to read Luke 8:1-3. Allow Mary to tell you the story in her words.

My name is Mary and I come from the town of Magdala. Like Peter, James and John, most everybody in the village is involved in the fishing industry. We're particularly noted for our smoked fish. The export business here is brisk. My family prospered in this town; you'd say we were quite well-to-do. But for me that was of no avail. I was so sick and no amount of money was finding me a cure. I don't know what name you'd give my ailment today, but in my day we talked about evil spirits as the cause. I was so bad off that they said I had seven demons. In our world "seven" is the perfect number—it signifies completeness. I was completely sick and had reached the end of my endurance.

One day, when I thought I couldn't take much more, people in town were all astir over a new healer. His name was Jesus and they were saying that everybody who touched him got better. What did I have to lose? I would say what happened to me when I met him was a miracle—he healed me completely! Not only that, but I listened to his teaching and I was spellbound by it. I couldn't resist him. I decided that all the money I had was of no use—what really mattered was the reign of God as he described it. I made up my mind to use my wealth to help him spread the Word.

There were other women who did the same. There was Susanna, and there was Joanna, Chuza's wife. This financing of Jesus' mission was a lot harder for her. Her husband was Herod's steward. She had no end of conflict trying to keep what she was doing from him. Most of the rest of us were widows who had some control over our finances. Some of us had inherited money from our fathers because we had no brothers; others of us earned our own money, or were widows who were now able to have more control over our lives. As you know, in our day, women had very little access to money and little say in how it was spent. There were a few of us privileged ones, however, who did.

Our ministry was a very important one. With a number of the men going off preaching and healing and leaving behind their families and livelihoods, there had to be some of us to help provide. Those of us who were widows were freer to travel around with the men on mission. This often raised eyebrows, but we managed to deflect their criticism.

One last thing I want to clear up: It bothers me that people keep confusing me with other women that Jesus healed or forgave. I wasn't the one who wept over Jesus' feet, displaying extravagant love after she had been forgiven (Luke 7:36-50); nor was I the one who anointed him for burial (Mark 14:3-9; Matthew 26:6-13; John 12:1-12); nor was I the adulterer they tried to stone (John 7:53-8:11). I've heard about those others, but to tell you the truth, people don't even know the names of some of those women. One thing I can assure you—it wasn't me. Some have the mistaken notion that I was a prostitute before I met Jesus, or that I was a notorious sinner.

Though I wouldn't claim to be perfect, I don't know how such slander got started. What I can tell you is that after I was healed by Jesus I spent the rest of my life financing his mission and I followed him all the way to the end. I was there when they crucified him (23:49); I saw where they buried him (23:55); and it was I who led the other women back to the tomb the morning we found it empty (24:1-11). One of the most painful moments for me was when the other disciples did not believe us—they thought we were telling idle tales (24:11). Although Luke won't tell you this, I want you to know that I continued to have a big role in the preaching mission after the Resurrection. Another Gospel writer, whose name nobody now remembers, and whose work didn't get included in the canon of the Scriptures, wrote about some of the conflicts we had.[3] The men had such a hard time believing that I, too, had seen the risen Christ and that he had also sent me to proclaim the Good News.

What gave us the power to carry on under so many obstacles was the experience we had on Pentecost day. We were all together in the upper room when the whole place shook and tongues, as of fire, appeared. It was a frightening moment, but afterward, all our fears vanished and we had a boldness we had not previously known. That was one of those turning points you don't forget. It also gave us a new ability to experiment with how to pool our possessions. Luke will tell you how he understood it. Pause now to read Acts 2:43-47.

Holding All Things in Common

As you can see, there was no uniform response to Jesus when it came to possessions. For the most part, the ones who left everything behind, like Simon, were those whose specific ministry demanded that they divest of their possessions. It was the itinerant preachers who had to leave home and family to spread the word to people not their own. Others, like Mary of Magdala, gave away their possessions gradually, using them to finance the mission. Others sold all they had and put the proceeds together, then took from the common fund whatever they needed. That was a great leveler in the community, though it wasn't all that easy to do. When Ananias and Sapphira, for example, lied to the community about their property, the consequences were dire (Acts 5:1-11).

However a disciple is moved to respond, one thing is clear: What a person does with his or her possessions is intimately linked with following Jesus. Material wealth can be a great stumbling block, as a person's energies are directed toward taking care of, protecting and increasing it. Jesus was clear that "where your treasure is, there your heart will be also" (12:34). Each disciple must wrestle with the question: What does Jesus ask of me?

For Reflection

- *How has God blessed you with material resources? Spend some time thinking about them and thanking God for them.*

- *What is God asking you to let go of? What stands in the way of deeper discipleship for you?*

- *What would happen if we had the courage to go forth defenseless and dependent on others?*

- *How can a different model of power, that of vulnerability and forgiving love, be a healing force for our world?*

Closing Prayer

Giver of all good gifts,
we praise you and thank you
for the abundant blessings
you have bestowed on us.

You give us the wonders of creation,
you grace us with the splendor of life itself.
You provide for all our needs,
bodily and spiritual.

Fill us with gratitude
and convert our hearts
from any greed or selfishness
toward seeking you as our only treasure.

Give us courage to let go,
give us compassion so to share,
give us passion for just distribution
of this earth's goods.

We trust in your endless providence,
You who emptied yourself to become one of us,
You who have counted our every hair
and who feeds our hungers with your very self.

Empty us, fill us, mold us to yourself,
use us as your vessels of compassion and justice.
Accept our grateful prayer. Amen.

Notes

[1] Lyrics of the hymn, "Take, Lord, Receive" by the St. Louis Jesuits
in *Earthen Vessels* (Phoenix, Ariz.: North American Liturgy
Resources, 1975). Words based on a prayer from the Spiritual
Exercises of Saint Ignatius, no. 234.

[2] Anthony de Mello, *The Song of the Bird* (New York: Doubleday, 1984), pp. 132-133.

[3] See "The Gospel of Mary" in *New Testament Apocrypha*, translated by Edgar Hennecke, 2 vols., W. Schneemelcher, ed. (Philadelphia: Westminster, 1963), pp. 342. See also Karen L. King, "The Gospel of Mary Magdalene," in *Searching the Scriptures: A Feminist Commentary*, vol. 2, E. Schüssler Fiorenza, ed. (New York: Crossroad, 1994), pp. 601-634.

Day Four
Sowing Subversive Seeds

Coming Together in the Spirit

There was a woman who wanted peace in the world
and peace in her heart and all sorts of good things,
but she was very frustrated. The world seemed to be
falling apart. She would read the papers and get
depressed. One day she decided to go shopping,
and she went into a mall and picked a store at
random. She walked in and was surprised to see
Jesus behind the counter. She knew it was Jesus,
because he looked just like the pictures she'd seen
on holy cards and devotional pictures. She looked
again and again at him, and finally she got up her
nerve and asked, "Excuse me, are you Jesus?"

"I am."

"Do you work here?"

"No," Jesus said, "I own the store."

"What do you sell in here?"

"Oh, just about anything!"

"Anything?"

"Yes, anything you want. What do you want?"

She said, "I don't know."

"Well," Jesus said, "Feel free, walk up and down
the aisles, make a list, see what it is you want, and
then come back and we'll see what we can do for
you."

She did just that—walked up and down the

aisles. There was peace on earth, no more war, no hunger or poverty, peace in families, no more drugs, harmony, clean air, careful use of resources. She wrote furiously. By the time she got back to the counter, she had a long list. Jesus took the list, skimmed through it, looked up at her and smiled, "No problem." And then he bent down behind the counter and picked out all sorts of things, stood up, and laid out a row of little packets.

The woman asked, "What are these?"

Jesus replied, "Seed packets. This is a catalog store."

She said, "You mean I don't get the finished product?" "No, this is a place of dreams. You come and see what it looks like, and I give you the seeds. You plant the seeds. You go home and nurture them and help them to grow and someone else reaps the benefits."

"Oh," she said. And she left the store without buying anything.[1]

Defining Our Thematic Context

When we step out on the Word of God, we let ourselves be found by God's strong loving arms, as we saw on Day Two. We strive to respond to the invitation to rest in God in constant prayer, as we experienced on Day One. Yesterday we tried to listen to God's invitation to release our grip on our material possessions, either to leave all behind, or to put it at the service of the mission. Today we step out in ways that seem nonsensical and absurd. We enter the world of the parables, where the Word turns out to be a subversive seed—one that can turn us upside down—if we let it.

Opening Prayer

God who startles us out of complacency,
Your Word puzzles and confounds us.
Like the disciples who begged you to explain the
    parables to them,
We long for clarity, and you give us paradox.

We struggle in your topsy-turvy world,
where to lose one's life is to gain it,
and where the way through death
is the way to glory.

Help us to live with the ambiguities
While knowing surely that you lead us.
Show us how to sow your subversive Word
Until all earth brings forth your harvest of justice
    and peace.

RETREAT SESSION FOUR

Listen to the voice of Jesus:

The ministry in Galilee was going pretty well. Mostly I had been concentrating on healing people. There were so many who were in need: people with leprosy who had been ostracized and left to suffer in isolation, people who were paralyzed and had to rely on others for everything, people who were possessed by demons who suffered miserably. Some of these, like Mary of Magdala, became my disciples and were invaluable to the advancement of the mission. It gave me such delight to be able to restore so many people to wholeness. The crowds got bigger every day as word spread about the healing I can bring. Still, I spent as much time as I could in prayer, thanking

God for the divine power working through me, interceding for these beloved ones, and relishing union with our Creator.

I sensed that it was time to begin teaching my followers how to make meaning out of their experiences with me. I had spoken at length one day to a crowd about the blessedness of those who are poor, hungry, weeping and hated. I tried to teach about love of enemies and not judging others. I'm not sure how much they understood. Then while pondering our Scriptures it occurred to me that there were very effective teachers who used parables to bring home a point forcefully.

I remember the incident with David and the prophet Nathan (2 Samuel 12:1-12). It was after David had sent Uriah to his death so that he could have Bathsheba. Nathan was very upset and didn't know how to confront the king in a way that he would accept. So, under the guise of asking David's advice, Nathan presented the case of two men: one rich with flocks and herds in great numbers; the other poor with only one little ewe lamb. Nathan embellished the tale with heart-warming details of how the poor man raised his single lamb with great care, giving it to drink from his own cup and having it sleep in his bosom, so that it was like a daughter to him. One day the rich man received a visitor, but rather than take one of his own animals for the meal, he took the poor man's lamb! King David became furious at the story Nathan told and quickly rendered the verdict, "As the LORD lives, the man who has done this deserves to die; he shall restore the lamb fourfold, because he did this thing, and because he had no pity" (2 Samuel 12:5-6). That's what Nathan had hoped he would say. He quickly shot back, "You are the man!" (12:7) and he spelled out David's offenses to his face. And the king was brought to repentance, just as Nathan had hoped.

As I recalled this incident, I was inspired to try this technique with my own teaching. I would begin with familiar images from everyday life, so that my hearers would be able to relate immediately to the story. I would draw images from everyday life—from the domestic world of women, from the commercial lives of fishermen and from the agricultural realities of farmers. Once having drawn them into the story, I would tell it with a startling twist, like Nathan. The idea would be not to tell stories that confirm life as it is, but to offer a different vision of how life could be in God's realm.

I would provoke them into thinking differently about who God is, about who they are in relation to God and to their neighbors. I wanted to use Nathan's technique of bringing people to the point of having to make their own judgment. I wouldn't give them pat answers, but would try to leave the stories open-ended so that those who listened would need to wrestle with the meaning and decide what demand it would make on them.

Ultimately, my parables would aim to convert them to new ways of thinking and acting. Of course, the open-endedness also meant that each parable could have a variety of interpretations, depending on which character you identify with and where you stand in everyday life. I would try to get people to listen with the ears of the poor or the most downtrodden. If, like Nathan, I could get the powerful ones to hear the plight of the poor, perhaps they could be converted to God's just ways. For the poor I wanted to convey a message of hope and reassurance that God has not forgotten them and loves them fiercely.

One of the first I told was this: "A sower went out to sow his seed; and as he sowed, some fell on the path and was trampled on, and the birds of the air ate it up. Some fell on the rock; and as it grew up, it withered for lack of moisture. Some fell among thorns, and the thorns grew with it and choked it. Some fell into good soil, and when it grew, it produced a hundredfold." Then I called out, "Let anyone with ears to hear listen!" (Luke 8:4-8)

As I expected, they had a hard time with this parable. They discussed it long and hard and finally asked me what it meant. I didn't want to explain it, but wanted them to struggle with it until they could come to a point of insight that would lead to greater conversion. I knew that there were some who would hear but never understand because of their hard hearts (8:10). They had worked out that the story was meant to say something about God and God's realm, not just about a sower and seed and soil and harvest. But they could not agree on its meaning and had come to me to mediate.

The Parable of the Seed

Some said they thought it was about the seed, which looks so tiny and ineffective, but eventually does bring forth a yield, after many setbacks. They know what it's like to clear rocks from the ground and to battle thorns and other weeds, only to have their crop wither. But they also know the delight of having seed sprout up in good soil and the joy of reaping the ensuing harvest. They decided the seed is like the Word of God, and the difficulties in getting some to accept it are like battling rocks and weeds and shallow soil. But just as the seed is eventually effective, so too, the Word will bring forth fruit in abundance. Some thought that I was recasting Isaiah 55:10-11, "For as the rain and the snow come down from heaven, and do not return there until they have watered the earth, making it bring forth and sprout, giving seed to the sower and bread to the eater, so shall my word be that goes out from my mouth; it shall not return to me empty, but it shall accomplish that which I purpose, and succeed

in the thing for which I sent it." Indeed, I think I may
have had that subconsciously in the back of my mind.
Those who preferred this interpretation found that it gave
them hope in the face of the meager results of my
preaching.

The Parable of the Harvest

Others of my followers were intrigued by the harvest.
What kind of yield is one-hundredfold? That's absurd!
An average yield is about seven and a half; a good one
might be tenfold; but one-hundredfold is absolutely
unimaginable! The staggering amount propelled them
into thinking of the end-time, not just an everyday
harvest here and now. They thought the harvest
represents the overflowing fullness of God that surpasses
all human measure, and that will only be completely
known at the end of the ages. The proponents of this
interpretation found that the parable lifted their spirits
with a vision of a hope-filled future. It gave them
encouragement while they await God's bringing all to
completion.

The Parable of the Soil

There were others of my disciples who were
convinced that the focus of the parable is the different
types of soil, and that the soil was a metaphor for the
different ways people received the Word. The rocky
ground and the thorns describe those who have all kinds
of obstacles to their hearing and accepting the Word:
worldly cares, temptations and preoccupation with riches
and earthly pleasures. All these things prevent the Word
from "taking root" in their lives and transforming them.
The good soil represents those who are able to embrace
the Word with a generous and good heart and bear fruit

through perseverance (8:15). The advocates of this interpretation insisted that it was necessary to do everything possible to ensure that they were tilling and fertilizing the "soil" of their heart so that they would be good, receptive soil for the Word. They, too, found a message of hope.

The Parable of the Sower

There is one more aspect I had hoped they would contemplate in this parable. In the figure of the profligate sower I wanted them to see how God so wants all to be drawn into life with us that the Word is extended to every person, no matter how incapable they seem to receive it. God's graciousness is so extravagant, that the opportunity to receive the Word is offered even where there seems no possibility of acceptance and conversion. No one is outside God's loving concern; all are invited to receive the Word.

This interpretation would prove more challenging to my disciples. It gave comfort to those who formerly had been marginalized or considered sinners who now found themselves accepted into a community of believers. But to those who thought themselves special, as chosen "good soil," it was disconcerting to think of all these "others" being equally loved and sought after by God. Later, when the mission would go out to the Gentiles, some of my fellow Jews, who have always gloried in their unique relationship with God, found this difficult to accept. At the end of the parable I slipped in an allusion to the prayer that we Jews all pray every day from Deuteronomy 6:4: "Hear O Israel! The LORD is our God, the LORD alone!" In saying, "Let anyone with ears to hear listen!" I was trying to open up the notion that the Word is now being extended to all, Jew and Gentile. Now any who hear may respond with faith.

The Message for You

So which interpretation is the "right" one? I never settled it for those first disciples, which caused them a bit of frustration. Actually, I was delighted that they understood it in all of the above ways. I wanted the parable to open up many avenues into God's realm. I invite you to ponder the parable anew. Ask God to show you the meaning it holds for you. Let yourself be startled or disturbed or puzzled by the story. Let it turn your expectations upside down and ask God to till the soil of your heart to receive the Word with a generous heart and to persevere in acting upon it.

Mighty Mustard

All my first followers knew what mustard was like—the tall shrub with its delicate yellow flower and pungent extract can be found everywhere in Palestine. It is the bane of a farmer's existence—once it gets into a field it is impossible to eradicate. To most it is an exasperating weed. As I searched one day for an apt image for the realm of God, it struck me how well a mustard seed would convey it. So I told this parable:

"What is the kingdom of God like? And to what should I compare it? It is like a mustard seed that someone took and sowed in the garden; it grew and became a tree, and the birds of the air made nests in its branches" (Luke 13:18-19).

They puzzled over that one for a long time. Mustard was very familiar. And so was the image of a tree with birds nesting in its branches. Not only was this latter image something they observed in nature, but it also resonated with the biblical image that the prophets used for all the nations dwelling in the shelter of Israel's "tree" in the end times. Ezekiel prophesied this in God's name:

"I myself will take a sprig from the lofty top of a
    cedar;
I will set it out.
I will break off a tender one from the topmost of its
    young twigs;
I myself will plant it on a high and lofty mountain.
On the mountain height of Israel I will plant it,
in order that it may produce boughs and bear fruit,
and become a noble cedar.
Under it every kind of bird will live;
in the shade of its branches will nest
winged creatures of every kind" (Ezekiel 17:22-23).

Backyard Weeds

What I wanted my disciples to understand was that
the realm of God was not something that had to be
imported from far away Lebanon, like the cedar that
Ezekiel talked about. Nor does the realm of God consist
in special, elaborate material. Cedar wood, of course, was
used for the building of our Temple in Jerusalem (1 Kings
5:8-10) and was always thought to be luxurious. Nor is
the one who brings God's reign a powerful king who will
charge in as a conquering hero.

Rather, like mustard, the realm of God is more like an
ordinary garden-variety weed that can be found right at
home, in every person's own backyard. I am bringing it to
them in the guise of an ordinary human being, with a
kind of power that is far different from that of warriors
on swift steeds or monument-building kings. The gospel
that I am preaching has a subversive power like that of
mustard. It resides in the faith of ordinary people who
accept the Word—and with this faith they have the power
to transform the whole world! Such tenacious faith, like
mustard, can never be eradicated once it has taken root.

I'm afraid they did not catch on to the whole of the

meaning of this until after I had completed my earthly work with them. Only after I had been crucified and risen did they begin to understand about this kind of power that appears vulnerable and weak, but reveals the true face of God's might.

Out of Control

One other point I was trying to convey with the mustard parable was the uncontrollable way that the Word spreads. Mustard respects no boundaries; it crosses into wheat fields and plots of barley indiscriminately. One who deliberately sows mustard, as in the parable I posed, would ordinarily be very careful to plant only a very limited amount, since it tends to grow wild and take over other patches. I was hoping this image would provoke my followers to reflect on the strict boundaries of their world, delineating clean and unclean; those in favor with God and those without. I have been inviting into God's realm all kinds of people: sick, sinners, those ostracized and many considered unclean. This has made some people uncomfortable. It challenges their whole view of what it means to be holy as God is holy (Leviticus 11:44). I tried another image that I thought would bring home this point from yet another angle.

Runaway Leaven[2]

I said to them, "To what should I compare the kingdom of God? It is like yeast that a woman took and hid in three measures of flour until all of it was leavened" (Luke 13:20-21).

The women disciples had an easier time with this parable than the men. I tried to use images from the worlds of both so they would understand that women and men are called equally into God's realm. What was more of a challenge was to stretch their imaginations to envision the work of God like the work of a woman. This is not something I made up; actually we have a number of other places in our Scriptures where God is spoken of in female terms, as I pointed out on Day Two.

Bakerwoman God

Moses, for example, once reminded the Israelites not to forget "the God who gave you birth" (Deuteronomy 32:18). Isaiah spoke about God's anguish over Israel like that of "a woman in labor" (Isaiah 42:14). Another time when Isaiah was trying to console Israel he spoke for God, "Can a woman forget her infant, be without tenderness for the child of her womb? Even should she forget, yet I will never forget you" (Isaiah 49:15).

These are only some of the instances in which our Scriptures speak of God in female images. But in our patriarchal culture, most people pictured God as male. Of course, all the language we use for God is metaphorical—that is, no image can ever convey all that God is. I tried, in my parables, to stretch the imagination of my disciples so that they could have a fuller understanding of God and to see that both women and men were equally made in God's image.

Party Baking

My disciples knew right away that this parable was meant to say more than just how a person prepares daily sustenance. They knew the story of Abraham's three heavenly visitors (Genesis 18:6) and that this same grandiose amount—three measures or fifty pounds—is what Sarah used to bake for them. Gideon used this amount, too, when preparing for an angel of God (Judges 6:19). So did Hannah when she prepared the offering for the presentation of Samuel in the temple at Shiloh (1 Samuel 1:24). In each of these well-known stories, the large-scale baking prepares for an epiphany—it is God who is coming to dinner!

'Corrupting' Yeast

There were other details in the parable that puzzled my first hearers. The leaven is paradoxical: while it is a good thing in bread, it always signifies something evil or corrupt when it appears in a saying or story. You modern readers say, "One bad apple spoils the barrel." In our day we would say, "A little yeast leavens the whole batch of dough." Paul would later use that in his letter to the Galatians (5:9) when he was warning them not to be misled by those preaching a false message. I would warn my disciples, "Beware of the yeast of the Pharisees, that is, their hypocrisy" (Luke 12:1).

The way yeast got to have this meaning is that at the Exodus our ancestors had to depart in haste from Egypt, with no time to wait for dough to be leavened. And so, in our Passover ritual we eat unleavened bread for seven days (Exodus 12:15-20,34). Eating unleavened bread became a sign of membership in God's holy people. So, too, our grain offerings were to be unleavened (Leviticus 2:11).

Holiness Turned Upside Down

Here's the twist, then: The reign of God is like a batch of dough that has been permeated through and through by what, according to our former standards, we would consider corruptive. God's realm thoroughly incorporates persons who would have been considered corrupt, unclean, or sinners. This subversive little parable reverses previous notions of holiness. Those who formerly stood on the margins and felt themselves unworthy of God's attention, can begin to see themselves as "leaven," the vital life-giving component of the believing community. For those who had always thought themselves part of the privileged people of God, there is a new challenge to accept those they previously considered "corrupt"—they are the very ones who provide the active ingredient for the growth of the community of God's people!

Beyond that, there is a further unsettling piece of this parable. After my death, when the Gospel would go forth to the Gentiles, the Jewish Christians would struggle even more with this notion. Having let a few Gentiles mix in with the community, like a little leaven in dough, these were now changing the character of the whole community. Their "corrupting" influence was having a disturbing effect on the whole Jewish understanding of God and their ways of living faithfully according to the Law. It is one thing to invite in one who is different and have them adopt our ways; it is quite another when they start "taking over" like runaway fermenting yeast.

Enlivening Agitation

I invite you to let this parable get under your skin, too. Who in your world do you consider "corrupt" yeast? What would it mean not only to incorporate them into your believing community, but to allow yourself to be transformed by them? Does your community struggle with female images of God and with decisions about women's work and ministries? Is opening the door to areas of ministry that have traditionally been closed to women like ruining the customary unleavened loaf, or does the agitating action of such "yeast" cause the whole loaf to rise and be transformed into fulfilling fare for the whole community?

For Reflection

- *As you ponder the parable of the seed/sower/soil/harvest, ask God to till the soil of your heart to become ever more receptive to the Word that is being sown there. Let yourself be cultivated by God's loving care. Listen to how God is asking you to respond in ways that will make you even more fertile ground for the Word.*

- *Focusing on the image of the "mighty mustard" reflect on your image of power. How have you experienced God's "power made perfect in weakness" (2 Corinthians 12:9)?*

- *In what ways do you sow "subversive seeds" that challenge the status quo, and like leaven, bring transformative energy for fullness of life for all in the realm of God?*

Closing Prayer

Christ Jesus, Word made flesh,
we thank you for the seed of the Word
that has taken root in our hearts.
We ask you to till the soil of our selves
to become ever more receptive to you.

We puzzle over your inscrutable ways
of inclusion and boundary-breaking.
Upturn our notions of holiness
so we may be transformed for life in God's realm.

Teach us your way of power through vulnerability,
as we see God revealed mightily in your crucifixion.
Help us live the paradoxes
as we, too, become subversive sowers of your Word.

Notes

[1] Megan McKenna, *Parables: The Arrows of God* (Maryknoll: Orbis, 1994), pp. 28-29.

[2] See also Reid, "A Woman Mixing Dough," in *Choosing the Better Part?*, pp. 169-178.

DAY FIVE

Dining in God's Realm

Coming Together in the Spirit

In her short story, "Revelation," Flannery O'Connor tells of Mrs. Ruby Turpin, a woman who prides herself on being a good woman who helps other people and is saved by Jesus. Mrs. Turpin had a clear hierarchy of the classes of people. On the bottom of the heap were "colored people." Then, just next to them, "white-trash." She and her husband, Claud, homeowners and landowners, were far above.

A disturbing incident in a doctor's waiting room, in which Mrs. Turpin is assaulted by a "lunatic" young woman, who calls her "a wart hog from hell," is followed by this vision at the edge of her hog pen:

> Until the sun slipped finally behind the tree line, Mrs. Turpin remained there with her gaze bent to them as if she were absorbing some abysmal life-giving knowledge. At last she lifted her head. There was only a purple streak in the sky, cutting through a field of crimson and leading, like an extension of the highway, into the descending dusk. She raised her hands from the side of the pen in a gesture hieratic and profound. A visionary light settled in her eyes. She saw the streak as a vast swinging bridge extending upward from the earth through a

field of living fire. Upon it a vast horde of souls were rumbling toward heaven. There were whole companies of white-trash, clean for the first time in their lives, and bands of black niggers in white robes, and battalions of freaks and lunatics shouting and clapping and leaping like frogs. And bringing up the end of the procession was a tribe of people whom she recognized at once as those who, like herself and Claud, had always had a little of everything and the God-given wit to use it right. She leaned forward to observe them closer. They were marching behind the others with great dignity, accountable as they had always been for good order and common sense and respectable behavior. They alone were on key. Yet she could see by their shocked and altered faces that even their virtues were being burned away. She lowered her hands and gripped the rail of the hog pen, her eyes small but fixed unblinkingly on what lay ahead. In a moment the vision faded but she remained where she was, immobile.

At length she got down and turned off the faucet and made her slow way on the darkening path to the house. In the woods around her the invisible cricket choruses had struck up, but what she heard were the voices of the souls climbing upward into the starry field and shouting hallelujah."[1]

Defining Our Thematic Context

We took one more step out on the Word of God in Day Four when we let the subversive seed of Jesus' paradoxical parables sink into the soil of our selves. As we persist in wrestling with the parables' meaning, we continue to walk in prayerful consciousness of God's all-encompassing love. We move now to dinner parties at which Jesus is either host or guest. Often Jesus' teaching takes place in a meal setting. There are startling things that happen when Jesus is coming for dinner. The guest list is surprising and the table conversation leaves some diners with indigestion! All culminates at the final supper Jesus shared with his disciples.

Opening Prayer

Prayer for a New Society

All-nourishing God, your children cry for help
Against the violence of our world:
Where children starve for bread and feed on
    weapons;
Starve for vision and feed on drugs;
Starve for love and feed on videos;
Starve for peace and die murdered in our streets.

Creator God, timeless preserver of resources,
Forgive us for the gifts that we have wasted.
Renew for us what seems beyond redemption;
Call order and beauty to emerge again from chaos.
Convert our destructive power into creative service;
Help us to heal the woundedness of our world.

Liberating God, release us from the demons of
    violence.
Free us today from the disguised demon of deterrence
That puts guns by our pillows and missiles in our
    skies.
Free us from all demons that blind and blunt our
    spirits;
Cleanse us from all justifications for violence and
    war;

Open our narrowed hearts to the suffering and the
poor.

Abiding God, loving renewer of the human spirit,
Unfold our violent fists into peaceful hands;
Stretch our sense of family to include our neighbors;
Stretch our sense of neighbor to include our enemies
Until our response to you finally respects and
embraces
All creation as precious sacraments of your presence.

Hear the prayer of all your starving children.[2]
Amen.

Retreat Session Five

Listen as Jesus recalls:

One of the first people that followed me was Levi
(Luke 5:27-32). He was a well-known figure in
Capernaum. He sat at his customs post each day,
collecting tariffs from all who crossed the borderline
between the territory of Antipas and that of Philip. He
didn't collect land taxes and poll tax—those were under
the direct supervision of the Roman prefects and
procurators. They had their own bureaucrats for that, and
not many of them were Jews. Levi's job was to collect
tolls, imposts, customs and tariffs. The way it worked was
that he paid the Romans in advance and then had to
recoup enough to make a profit to be able to live.

Like all toll collectors, Levi was despised by his own
people. There were several reasons for this. Some Jews
thought toll collectors to be turncoats by working for the
Romans. Plus, by having constant contact with Gentiles,

he was always ritually impure. But most of all, toll collectors were widely accused of cheating their own people in order to line their own pockets.

But what you must understand is that these were hard times and people did what they could out of desperation. No self-respecting Jew would go looking for such a job unless it was the last resort. Toll collectors were just low-level functionaries who had no bargaining power and could be replaced at the drop of a hat. But at least there was the hope that he could earn enough to feed his family.[3]

I never asked Levi what brought him to this point, whether he'd lost his land because of famine or sickness or pestilence—anything like that can happen in such precarious times. But I could see the goodness in him and his struggle to be honest in a job he detested. When he decided to follow me, we celebrated at a great dinner he hosted. All the other Jewish toll collectors were there— who else would associate with him?

I knew that many would not agree with my decision to go to Levi's house. We have very strict boundaries in our tradition of who eats with whom, where, when, what is served and how it is prepared. Like eats with like. But it had become clear to me that dinner settings were the perfect place to begin to make God's realm more visible here and now. Hadn't our prophet Isaiah seen this, too, when he described the messianic times this way?

> On this mountain the Lord of hosts will make for all
>   peoples
> a feast of rich food, a feast of well-aged wines,
> of rich food filled with marrow, of well-aged wines
>   strained clear (Isaiah 25:6).

It seemed to me that the only way God's love would reach those who were on the margins was by sitting down together with them, not by keeping separate from them. Rather than fear that I would be contaminated by their sin, would they not instead be changed by my offer of forgiveness and salvation?

The Extravagant Guest

There was another time I remember clearly. I had been invited to dine with Simon, a Pharisee (Luke 7:36-50). I'm still not sure why he asked me to come, whether he was trying to test me or whether he was just curious about me. I don't think he was expecting what happened. We were all reclining at table, when in came a woman I had encountered a few days before. I remembered her well. She had been overcome with joy when I assured her that her sins were forgiven. She found her way into Simon's house. It was customary to put out leftovers for the poor after a big banquet, so it wasn't hard for her to gain entrance.

She had with her a lovely alabaster flask of ointment that had the most delightful fragrance. She made her way over to where I was and began to caress my feet. This was a fancy dinner and we were all stretched out on cushions, leaning on our left elbows, reaching with our right hands for the dishes of food near our heads, so it was easy for her to kneel at my feet. She broke the little flask of ointment and poured it over my feet. Then, she began to weep and her tears mingled with the ointment. She then loosened her beautiful long hair and began to wipe my feet with it. She was so beautiful and her love was so genuine. I couldn't help but feel like the bridegroom in the Song of Songs who extolled the charms of his bride-to-be,

> How beautiful you are, my love,
> how very beautiful!

> Your eyes are doves
> behind your veil.
> Your hair is like a flock of goats,
> moving down the slopes of Gilead
> (Song of Songs 4:1).

It gave me extreme pleasure to see the way she was so
open to God's love and mine. She didn't seem at all
aware that my host was glaring at her and grumbling to
himself that I could hardly be a prophet if I did not know
that she was a sinner and let her touch me this way.
Couldn't Simon see that her lavish gestures to me were
evidence of the love that fills her now that she knows she
is forgiven? How would I make him see this?

I turned to Simon and posed this for his
consideration:

> A certain creditor had two debtors; one owed five
> hundred denarii, and the other fifty. When they
> could not pay, he canceled the debts for both of
> them. Now which of them will love him more?"
> Simon answered, "I suppose the one for whom he
> canceled the greater debt" (Luke 7:41-43).

With a fictitious example, he got the point straight away.
The big question was, what about the genuine example
right in front of his eyes? So I turned to her while I asked
Simon, "Do you see this woman?" (7:44). Silence. Doesn't
he get it? I tried prompting him, showing him what I had
seen in her deeds, which were so different from his own.

> Then turning toward the woman, he said to Simon,
> "Do you see this woman? I entered your house; you
> gave me no water for my feet, but she has bathed
> my feet with her tears and dried them with her hair.
> You gave me no kiss, but from the time I came in
> she has not stopped kissing my feet. You did not
> anoint my head with oil, but she has anointed my

feet with ointment. Therefore, I tell you, her sins, which were many, have been forgiven; hence she has shown great love. But the one to whom little is forgiven, loves little" (Luke 7:44-47).

I desperately wanted him to see that her lavish love toward me was her way of expressing how joy-filled and free she is ever since she experienced my forgiveness some days ago. Couldn't he see that he himself was also in need of the forgiveness I could offer? Granted, his sins were fewer, but nonetheless, I could free him to be more loving. If he could still see her only as a sinner and not as the beautiful, loving, freed woman she now is, how would he ever understand who I am?

I left the dinner that night a bit discouraged. Simon seemed to be listening more to his friends who were murmuring under their breath, "Who is this who even forgives sins?" (Luke 7:49). But I will nourish the hope that he will at some point be ready to respond with faith in me.

A Universal Guest List

This wasn't the last time I ate with a Pharisee. One sabbath I accepted another invitation from a leading Pharisee. I had the feeling that everybody was watching me closely, but not in a friendly manner! One of the people in front of me was in obvious distress. He was suffering from dropsy. I looked at him and knew that he wanted to be healed. But I also knew I would draw the ire of the scholars of the law and all the Pharisees at table. So I posed the question straight to them, "Is it lawful to cure people on the sabbath, or not?" (Luke 14:3). They said nothing.

I attended to the man with dropsy. He had the faith to be healed right away; afterward I sent him on his way. I could feel all the judgmental eyes boring into me. So I

simply asked, "If one of you has a child or an ox that has
fallen into a well, will you not immediately pull it out on
a sabbath day?" (Luke 14:5). They didn't answer, but I
think they got my point.

Just then dinner was served, and as everyone moved
toward the table, I watched how they all juggled for the
places of honor. I also saw how they only invited their
friends and those in their own social circle. This is typical,
but it will never do in God's realm. I tried to tell them
about it, again in parable form:

> Someone gave a great dinner and invited many. At
> the time for the dinner he sent his slave to say to
> those who had been invited, "Come; for everything
> is ready now." But they all alike began to make
> excuses. The first said to him, "I have bought a piece
> of land, and I must go out and see it; please accept
> my regrets." Another said, "I have bought five yoke
> of oxen, and I am going to try them out; please
> accept my regrets." Another said, "I have just been
> married, and therefore I cannot come." So the slave
> returned and reported this to his master. Then the
> owner of the house became angry and said to his
> slave, "Go out at once into the streets and lanes of
> the town and bring in the poor, the crippled, the
> blind, and the lame." And the slave said, "Sir, what
> you ordered has been done, and there is still room."
> Then the master said to the slave, "Go out into the
> roads and lanes, and compel people to come in, so
> that my house may be filled. For I tell you, none of
> those who were invited will taste my dinner" (Luke
> 14:16-24).

I wanted my fellow diners to see that the kinds of people
they invite to their dinners are selfish, obsessed with their
property and intent on acquiring more. I tried to unmask
the game of one-upsmanship they are playing every time
they have a banquet. I wanted them to try to see what

would happen if the whole thing blew up. There were two ways of looking at what would happen to the host in my story: Either you see him as ruined socially, or you realize he is now a free man.

This is no idle tale. A number of my followers have had to come to grips with this very issue. Not everyone who follows me is poor and marginalized. There are also some well-to-do folks among my disciples. It is a great dilemma for them: Can they still maintain their elite status and their former circle of friends, clients and associates if they are also associating with the more rag-tag members of my community? And for the ones of lower status, it is no less uncomfortable. They know they don't belong with the upper strata; they feel out of place, under-dressed, unsure of how to behave. They have to be compelled to sit down with the upper crust. How will my followers work it out so that all are welcome at the same table, as a living sign that all are received into God's realm?

The Last Supper

It had become more and more clear to me that the authorities wouldn't tolerate me much longer. I knew this even before we went to Jerusalem. In fact, that time I went off into the hills to pray after we had fed the five thousand, I had a profound experience of union with the Creator (Luke 9:28-36). I had been wrestling with the urge to go to the Holy City, so that my message might reach to the heart of our religious leadership. But I was fully aware that Jerusalem is the city that always kills prophets (Luke 13:34). And then it came to me! In the midst of my prayer, I saw clearly that it was precisely through my death that my mission would be accomplished. My death would be a new Exodus—a new liberation of my people. The sure direction and profound oneness with God that I had that day would remain a touchstone for me in the dreadful moments ahead. It gave me the strength to be able to love all the way to my death.

We were in Jerusalem for the Passover feast and I was fortunate enough to get us a large upper room where I could celebrate with my disciples. It was a bittersweet night. I sensed that tonight might be my last with them, yet ritual carried us into exuberant celebration. I still had so much to tell them. I wanted them to remember all that I had tried to teach them and to live as I had tried to show them. I said to them, "I have eagerly desired to eat this Passover with you before I suffer; for I tell you, I will not eat it until it is fulfilled in the kingdom of God." Then I took a cup, and after giving thanks I said, "Take this and divide it among yourselves; for I tell you that from now on I will not drink of the fruit of the vine until the kingdom of God comes." Then I took a loaf of bread, and gave thanks, broke it, and gave it to them, saying, "This is my body, which is given for you. Do this in remembrance of me." And I did the same with the cup after supper, saying, "This cup that is poured out for you is the new covenant in my blood" (Luke 22:15-20).

I wanted them to understand that they were not just to do the ritual in my memory, but to live as I had shown them. I wanted them to be ready to follow my way of love to the death, even for those who would not love them back. I so hoped that in the tumultuous events of the next three days they would begin to understand what I had said earlier to them about loving even their enemies. It's easy to love those who love you. But could they find the ways to respond to violence and insult with loving, nonviolent confrontation? Could they do good even to those who hate them? Could they pray for those who mistreat them?

Such tactics do not let injustice go unconfronted; I

don't want them to be like doormats that oppressors can walk all over. I want them to learn a different kind of strength than military might. I want them to know the power of the Spirit that will help them confront a wrongdoer with love in such a way that will bring that one to repentance. I want them to look for opportunities to perform acts of kindness to those outside their own circle of friends and kin. That is how my God acts; that is how I tried to teach them to act.

I knew they would need one another to support such efforts. My deepest hope was that their table celebrations in my memory would be done in such a way that they would know me present with them again and again. Every time they would eat of the bread and drink of the cup I wanted them to be able to be in intimate communion with me. My dearest dream was that they could do this in inclusive communities where all social, gender, racial, ethnic and any other distinctions were dissolved so they could all be one in my love. Was it too much to hope?

For Reflection

- *How do I cross boundaries of gender, race, ethnicity, age, disability, religion, sexual preference, or social status?*

- *What kinds of inclusivity are easiest for me? Which are hardest for me? How can I grow in showing God's all-inclusive embrace? What would be the cost? What freedom would it bring?*

- *How do I respond to those who mistreat me? How can I grow in Jesus' way of nonviolent, loving confrontation?*

Closing Prayer

Come, Let us Celebrate
Come,
Let us celebrate the supper of the Lord.
Let us make a huge loaf of bread
and let us bring abundant wine
like at the wedding of Cana.

Let the women not forget the salt.
Let the men bring along the yeast.
Let many guests come,
the lame, the blind, the crippled, the poor.

Come quickly.
Let us follow the recipe of the Lord.
All of us, let us knead the dough together
with our hands.
Let us see with joy
how the bread grows.

Because today
we celebrate
the meeting with the Lord.
Today we renew our commitment
to the Kingdom.
Nobody will stay hungry.[4]

Notes

1 Flannery O'Connor, "Revelation," in *The Complete Stories* (New York: Farrar, Straus and Giroux, 1971), pp. 508-509.

2 "Prayer for a New Society" from Pax Christi USA, 348 East Tenth Street, Erie, PA 16503-1110.

3 On the tax system in Roman Palestine see John R. Donahue, "Tax Collectors and Sinners: An Attempt at Identification," *CBQ* 33

(1971), pp. 39-61; William R. Herzog II, *Parables as Subversive Speech* (Louisville: Westminster/John Knox, 1994), pp. 180-184.

[4] By Elsa Tamez, in *Women's Prayer Services*, ed. by Iben Gjerding and Katherine Kinnamon (Mystic, Conn.: Twenty-Third Publications, 1987), p. 20.

DAY SIX
Choosing the Better Part

Coming Together in the Spirit

Sojourner Truth, an African-American woman and
former slave, who could not read or write, addressed
these words to a suffrage gathering in Akron, Ohio, in
1852:

> That man over there say
> a woman needs to be helped into carriages
> and lifted over ditches
> and to have the best places everywhere.
> Nobody ever helped me into carriages
> or over mud puddles
> or give me best place...
> And ain't I a woman?
> Look at me!
> Look at my arm!
> I have plowed and planted
> and gathered into barns
> and no man could head me...
> And ain't I a woman?
> I could work as much
> and eat as much as a man—
> when I could get it—
> and bear the lash as well,
> and ain't I a woman?

I have borne 13 children
and seen most all sold into slavery
and when I cried out a mother's grief
none but Jesus heard me...
and ain't I a woman?
That little man in black there say
a woman can't have as much rights as a man
cause Christ wasn't a woman.
Where did your Christ come from?
From God and a woman!
Man had nothing to do with him!
If the first woman God ever made
was strong enough to turn the world
upside down, all alone
together women ought to be able to turn it
rightside up again.[1]

Defining Our Thematic Context

Men and women, slave and free, Jew and Gentile struggled in the early Church to learn how to step out on the Word of God together. The challenges that faced them were enormous. The cultural, social and religious scripts of the first-century Mediterranean world dictated differing roles based on these categories of distinction. In this sixth day of our retreat we reflect together on the struggle of the early believers to truly embody Jesus' all-inclusive vision. While the focus will be on the interplay between women and men disciples, I invite you to extend these reflections to the struggles we face in the Church and society in our own day for equality and inclusivity, not only with regard to gender distinctions, but those based on race, ethnicity, sexual orientation, or any other difference.

Opening Prayer

A Litany of Women for the Church

Dear God, creator of women in your own image,
born of a woman in the midst of a world half women,
carried by women to mission fields around the globe,
made known by women to all the children of the
    earth,
give to the women of our time
the strength to persevere,
the courage to speak out,
the faith to believe in you beyond
all systems and institutions
so that your face on earth may be seen in all its
    beauty,
so that men and women become whole,
so that the church may be converted to your will
in everything and in all ways.

We call on the holy women
who went before us,
channels of Your Word
in testaments old and new,
to intercede for us
so that we might be given the grace
to become what they have been
for the honor and glory of God.

Saint Esther, who pleaded against power for the
    liberation of the people,   *Pray for us.*
Saint Judith, who routed the plans of men and saved
    the community,
Saint Deborah, laywoman and judge, who led the
    people of God,
Saint Elizabeth of Judea, who recognized the value
    of another woman,

Saint Mary Magdalene, minister of Jesus, first
evangelist of the Christ,

Saint Scholastica, who taught her brother Benedict to
honor the spirit above the system,

Saint Hildegard, who suffered interdict for the doing
of right,

Saint Joan of Arc, who put no law above the law of
God,

Saint Clare of Assisi, who confronted the pope with
the image of woman as equal,

Saint Julian of Norwich, who proclaimed for all of us
the motherhood of God,

Saint Thérèse of Lisieux, who knew the call to
priesthood in herself,

Saint Catherine of Siena, to whom the pope listened,

Saint Teresa of Avila, who brought women's gifts to
the reform of the church,

Saint Edith Stein, who brought fearlessness to faith,

Saint Elizabeth Seton, who broke down the
boundaries between lay women and religious by
wedding motherhood and religious life,

Saint Dorothy Day, who led the church to a new
sense of justice,

* * *

Mary, mother of Jesus, who heard the call of God and
answered,   *Pray for us.*

Mary, mother of Jesus, who drew strength from the
woman Elizabeth,

Mary, mother of Jesus, who underwent hardship
bearing Christ,

Mary, mother of Jesus, who ministered at Cana,

Mary, mother of Jesus, inspirited at Pentecost,

Mary, mother of Jesus, who turned the Spirit of God
into the body and blood of Christ, pray for us. Amen.[2]

Retreat Session Six

When I, Luke, was composing my Gospel, I was aware that there were many more stories about women disciples than Mark included in his Gospel. And in my day, women continued to play very important roles in our believing community. I thought it essential to include these traditions, not only for the women believers, but as inspiration and guide for the men as well. I must admit, though, that we were not all of the same mind about what roles were proper for women Christians.

It was undeniable that there were women who Jesus called to follow him and who shared his mission. I already introduced you to Mary Magdalene, Joanna and Susanna on Day Three. But what were proper ministries for women in our day? That was not an easy question to answer. We had heard about some unusual practices. In Cenchreae, the port city of Corinth, Phoebe was leading the community as deacon and patron (Romans 16:1-2) and was entrusted by Paul with his crucial letter for the Church in Rome. Also in Corinth, Paul had befriended Prisca and Aquila (Acts 18), a husband and wife team who together led the Church that met in their house (Romans 16:3-5) and who traveled with him to minister in Ephesus (Acts 18:18-19). In Philippi, Lydia was the first convert and head of the community (Acts 16:11-15, 40). In due time Euodia and Syntyche became influential evangelists and leaders there, too (Philippians 4:2-3). Nympha was head of the house Church in Colossae (Colossians 4:15) and Junia was a notable apostle (Romans 16:7).

Still, there were plenty of people in the communities who found this very upsetting. Some insisted that women should keep silent in church (1 Corinthians 14:34) and that women should only teach other women (Titus 2:3-4).

For some, it was all right if women led the gatherings inside the home, but they deemed it improper for women to represent the community in public. Some Christians were afraid of being too different from the surrounding culture; they were afraid of drawing unwanted attention from the authorities. In some places Christians were suffering persecution and it was better not to stand out.

For myself, I highly prize the commitment and gifts of the women in our communities and I tried to bring that out in the way I told their stories. The question of women in leadership roles is still a thorny one for us. I will let them tell you their own stories now. I hope that as you reflect on our struggles it may guide you in how to respond to the ones you face in your day. We will begin with Mary and Martha. Pause to read Luke 10:38-42.

Ministering Sisters

I am Martha and I was always happy when Jesus would come to stay with us. The conversation was never dull and the disciples he would bring with him were always interesting. Some of them were regulars: Peter, James, John, Mary Magdalene, Joanna and Susanna were almost always with him. Others would come once but not the next time. We were happy to give hospitality to all who crossed our threshold.

I remember one time in particular when Jesus and the disciples had been on the road preaching the Good News to many villages. They were hot and tired when they arrived. I was happy I was home to receive them. Many days I would be out ministering to people in need. Sometimes it would be hungry people that had to be fed or sick people that needed medical attention. Of course, when the physical needs were taken care of people were ready to hear what we would have to say about Jesus and his message. It was a very satisfying ministry.

One disturbing thing, though, were the rumblings about women "gallavanting" around outside the home and the increasingly sharp criticisms toward us ministering women. There was dissension in the community about it. Some thought that a woman's only place is in her own home, tending her husband and children. Others quite approved of Mary of Magdala, Joanna, Susanna and the other women who traveled about Galilee, ministering with Jesus, and they encouraged all of us women to continue our ministries. I often wished that our critics would have come with us for a day to see all the good that we accomplished!

The widows came in for a little less criticism. A woman who had been married and had already raised her family and children did not come under quite the same suspicion. We tried to go in twos, as Jesus suggested (Luke 10:1) so that there would be less murmuring. There also began a new movement of ministering widows living together. Tabitha (some knew her by her Greek name, Dorcas [Acts 9:36-43]), for one, was an especially good seamstress and had organized a whole ministry to clothe the poor. But even these respectable and pious women came in for criticism.

There were some in the Church who wanted to recognize officially only those widows who were over sixty and who were married only once (1 Timothy 5:9). Hardly any could meet those requirements. Most of us married young and remarried if our first husbands died. It was upsetting to see the church not wanting to give financial support to the ministry of widows. Some were of a mind that those who had children and grandchildren could get their support from their family (1 Timothy 5:3-4). Others thought that the women who sponsored houses of widows ought to be the ones to assume their financial support (1 Timothy 5:16).

At any rate, things were coming to a head about women's roles in ministry in our community and many of us were very upset about it that night Jesus came with his disciples. As always, I welcomed him warmly and then we sat to listen to him. We told him how we had been experiencing such success in bringing people to faith in him. As always, it was a thrill to have him with us, to further instruct us and to encourage us in our ministries. Mary, my sister, always liked to sit at his feet, as disciples are wont to do. She wasn't saying anything to Jesus about our latest conflicts, but I was so agitated about it, that I finally let it all spill out.

I told him how, despite the great ways in which the Spirit was working through us, there were some of our own community who were getting more vociferous in their objections to women ministering outside the home. They were gathering more and more supporters who were increasingly putting obstacles in our way. It was getting unbearable for me, as some of the most actively involved women were backing away from visible ministries just to avoid conflict. Even my sister Mary was leaving me alone in the ministry! I asked Jesus to tell her to come back to help me and to guide us in knowing what to do.

He listened sympathetically and urged us not to get discouraged. He repeated to us what he had been telling all his disciples so many times, that we were to follow in his way as "one who serves" (Luke 22:27). He recommended that we try to be understanding and loving toward our opponents and to pray for them even as we pressed forward with our good work of ministry. He shared how often he, too, had encountered opposition. His way of envisioning God's reign and how we relate to one another in it is so hard for some to accept! We were greatly buoyed up by his peaceful spirit, and his way of being able to speak the truth in love when in the midst of conflict.

What distresses me now, however, is the way the story of that visit has been passed on to you modern-day readers of the Gospel. I have the utmost respect for Luke, and I appreciate the way he tried to highlight the stories of us women disciples. But he had his own agenda, too, you know. And it shows in the way he slanted the story. Worse yet is how Christians through the ages have misunderstood the whole episode. Many have thought that our struggle was in trying to keep a good balance between contemplative prayer and active ministry and that Jesus was encouraging us to choose the former over the latter. While every disciple feels the tension of wanting to pray more, while being pulled to respond to the urgent needs, I never knew Jesus to pit one against the other. In fact, he told us over and over that a good disciple is one who both hears the word and then puts it into practice (Luke 8:15; 11:28).

You can see how transmitters of the tradition have struggled with Luke's version of our story which seems to have Jesus take Mary's part so definitively against me. Scribes copying the manuscripts kept trying to fix verse 42. Some tried to soften the absolute pronouncement that Luke put on Jesus' lips and they wrote instead, "there is need of *only a few things*." Others combined this version with the original and wrote, "But of a few things there is need, or of one," which ends up nonsense. Some just left out the verse entirely.

What surprises me is how often readers of the Gospel think that the conflict is over what to have for dinner or who's getting it ready! They mistakenly think that the *"diakonia"* (10:40) about which I'm upset is "serving" the meal. In actuality, we were using *"diakonia"* to describe all kinds of ministerial service. In addition to serving at table

(Acts 6:2), it also meant ministry of the word (Acts 6:4), apostolic ministry (Acts 1:25), financial administration (Luke 8:3; Acts 11:29; 12:25), leadership (Luke 22:25-27), or ministry in general (Acts 20:24; 21:19).

Some modern interpreters think Jesus was being revolutionary by letting Mary sit at his feet, that he was unusual in promoting theological education for women. But these people miss the point, too. Jesus was not the only Jew who thought women should be educated in Torah.[3] Granted, most women had little time to study after caring for their responsibilities to family and household administration, but there were some. The real issue, as I have told you, was not that women heard the Word at Jesus' feet, but rather, what we would *do* with that Word. I'm afraid it was never fully resolved in my day. And I suspect that contemporary readers still have a long way to go in settling the issue. As you reflect on your cultural mores and ministerial demands, let the words and example of Jesus and his first women followers give you encouragement to follow the lead of the Spirit in your day to choose "the better part."

A Liberated Woman

Pause now to read Luke 13:10-17 and let this woman tell you her story.

It was a sabbath like any other. As I had done all my life, I hobbled into the synagogue to pray. Every step had become more and more difficult with the passing of the years. It was especially awful when people would not see me, bent over as I was. They would frequently knock me over. Knowing that they did not do it maliciously did not lessen the pain or the humiliation. It was also a source of great sadness to me that I could no longer look my friends and relatives in the eye. And it was rare that anyone would stoop down to converse face-to-face with me. But I did derive comfort from going to synagogue to pray. I would repeat over and over these verses from Psalm 5:

> But I, through the abundance of your steadfast love,
> will enter your house,
> I will bow down toward your holy temple
> in awe of you.
> Lead me, O Lord, in your righteousness
> because of my enemies;
> make your way straight before me (Psalm 5:6-7).

I thought of myself bowing down in reverence toward God day in and day out, while I earnestly trusted that God would make the way straight for me.

On this particular sabbath Jesus was teaching as I came in. I did not mean for him to see me. Before I could slip into a quiet corner he called out, "Woman you are set free from your infirmity!" And then he laid his hands on my back and I could feel the energy flowing from him into my whole spine. Without pain or effort I was able to straighten up for the first time in eighteen years. "Glory be to God!" I called out again and again! I could look at Jesus face to face! I will never forget how he gazed at me with such love. But I could also see that all the burden I had carried was now borne on his own shoulders. I remembered the prophecy of Isaiah, "I gave my back to those who struck me, and my cheeks to those who pulled out the beard; I did not hide my face from insult and spitting" (Isaiah 50:6). And in a flash, I knew that he would suffer greatly for what he had done for me that day.

The uproar began immediately. The leader of the synagogue was indignant and started to incite the crowd of worshipers. He kept shouting at Jesus that no work was to be done on the sabbath and to me he screamed,

"Come some other day to be cured!" I was so taken aback! I didn't come to be cured. I only came to pray! But how I could pray now standing straight and giving God full praise!

Jesus was quick in his response. He could see right through the hypocrisy. All of them untie their oxen and asses to feed them on the sabbath, so why shouldn't he untie me from my bondage to this satanic affliction on the holy day? In fact, what better time to be set free? His persuasive remarks won over the crowd and they joined me in praising God. The synagogue official simmered with humiliation. He couldn't see beyond the broken rule to God's delight in regenerating this broken body of mine.

From that day forward, I had a new appreciation for our ancestors' struggle at the Exodus. I likened their yoke of oppression under the Egyptians to the bondage I had experienced with my disability. The Pharaoh who was never quite ready to let our people go seemed so like our synagogue leader who thought Jesus' timing all wrong. I think God can only take the cries of overburdened people so long before the weight becomes intolerable and God must intervene and rescue. I suppose there will always be those who find fault with the timing. But is there ever a convenient time for liberation?

A Persistent Widow

Pause now to read Luke 18:1-8. I invite you to hear the widow tell her side of the story.

What was I to do? I couldn't tolerate the injustice any longer. I had to take action myself. Everybody thinks of widows as so helpless, the ones for whom everybody else has to care (Deuteronomy 24:17-22; Isaiah 10:2). But they underestimate the power of us "little people!" And all my experience of God encouraged me. Every story I've heard from our Scriptures has God taking the side of the oppressed—how could I lose with God on my side?

I knew the kinds of odds I faced. I knew the judge's reputation. He was about as far from what we'd want in a judge as you could get. This one was nothing like the judges Jehoshaphat appointed who were impartial, took no bribes, and had the fear of God, knowing they were judging on behalf of God (2 Chronicles 19:6-7). This one prided himself on having neither fear of God nor respect for any person. I didn't have any money to bribe him—so I would have little chance even of getting a hearing, much less a favorable verdict. I'd have to use unconventional tactics.

So I went day after day after day after day, demanding justice. He resisted for a long time. But I have nothing but time. So back I would go every morning. He tried to ignore me. He tried stopping his ears and turning away his face. He tried having me carried away. I always went back the next day. I knew eventually I would wear him out. I think he was actually beginning to be afraid that I'd resort to physical violence.[4] Many poor people do, when they get so frustrated with the system that won't listen to them. But it's rather ludicrous to imagine that I could get anywhere with violence. No, I relied on patience and on God-like persistence. I thought of all the times God had waited and persisted in enduring our unfaithfulness as the covenanted people. God never gave up on us until we would be drawn back with bands of love into the divine embrace. That's how I'd try to win over this impervious judge.

I could see that I was finally getting to him. And, at last, he gave in! I felt proud to follow in the footsteps of widows like Ruth and Tamar, two of our foremothers who were able to ensure the continuation of our lineage, by their heroic acts. Of course, my actions won't have such a grand-scale impact. I know I won't bring down the whole corrupt system this judge has set in place. I didn't convert him. But I did get one small victory for justice. Who knows? Maybe if all the seemingly powerless "little" people were to cry out together for justice, day after day after day, the systems of injustice would, indeed, topple.

For Reflection

- *How can we find the liberating way of Jesus amidst conflicting traditions? How can the struggles of the early Christian communities help us to hear and follow the Spirit's promptings in our own day?*

- *Are you carrying a burden that is weighing you down? Ask for God's touch to lift it now so that you can stand upright and glorify God. What kinds of societal bondage must be loosed? How can Christians act with God's urgency to liberate?*

- *What persistent, loving acts of confrontation can you engage in so as to be a God-like voice for justice until each small victory is won?*

Closing Prayer

A Litany of Women's Power

Spirit of Life, we remember today the women, named and unnamed,
who throughout time have used the power and gifts you gave them to change the world.
We call upon these foremothers to help us discover within ourselves your power—and the ways to use it to bring about the Kingdom of Justice and Peace.

We remember Sarah who with Abraham answered
God's call to forsake her homeland and put their
faith in a covenant with the Lord.
We pray for her power of faith.

We remember Esther and Deborah, whose acts of
individual courage saved their nation.
We pray for their power of courage to act for the
greater good.

We remember Mary Magdalene, and the other women
who followed Jesus who were not believed when
they announced the resurrection.
We pray for their power of belief in the face of
skepticisim.

We remember Phoebe, Priscilla, and the other women
leaders of the early church.
We pray for their power to spread the Gospel and
inspire congregations.

We remember the Abbesses of the Middle Ages who
kept faith and knowledge alive.
We pray for their power of leadership.

We remember Teresa of Avila and Catherine of Siena
who challenged the corruption of the Church
during the Renaissance.
We pray for their powers of intelligence and
outspokenness.

We remember [pray here for contemporary women
who have influenced your faith life].

We remember our own mothers and grandmothers
whose lives shaped ours.
We pray for the special power they attempted to pass
on to us.

We pray for the women who are victims of violence in
their homes.

May they be granted the power to overcome fear and
   seek solutions.

We pray for those women who face a life of poverty
   and malnutrition.
May they be granted the power of hopefulness to
   work together for a better life.

We pray for the women today who are "firsts" in
   their fields.
May they be granted the power to persevere and
   open up new possibilities for all women.

We pray for our daughters and granddaughters.
May they be granted the power to seek that life which
   is uniquely theirs.

We pray for [here add whomever else you wish].

We have celebrated the power of many women past
   and present.
It is time now to celebrate ourselves.
Within each of us is that same life and light and love.
Within each of us lie the seeds of power and glory.
Our bodies can touch with love;
Our hearts can heal;
Our minds can seek out faith and truth and justice.
Spirit of Life, be with us in our quest.[5] Amen.

Notes

[1] Quoted by Elizabeth Schüssler Fiorenza, *Jesus: Miriam's Child,
Sophia's Prophet* (New York: Continuum, 1994), pp. 57-58, from
Erlene Stetson, ed., *Black Sister: Poetry by Black American Women,
1746-1980* (Bloomington, Ind.: Indiana University Press, 1981),
pp. 24-25.

[2] By Joan Chittister, O.S.B., Benedictine Sisters, 355 East Ninth Street,
Erie, PA 16503.

[3] Philo of Alexandria, in *Vit. Cont.* 68, describes women ascetics, the *Therapeutides*, who dedicated their lives to study of Torah. And *m.Sota* 3:4 records the opinion of Ben Azzai, "A man ought to give his daughter a knowledge of the Law." Similarly, *m.Ned.* 4:3 declares it a religious duty to educate sons and daughters. There is also epigraphical evidence that Jewish women were leaders of synagogues, which would presume education in Torah. See Bernadette Brooten, *Women Leaders in the Ancient Synagogue: Inscriptional Evidence and Background Issues* (Brown Judaic Studies 36; Chico, Cal.: Scholars Press, 1982).

[4] The *NRSV* translation of verse 5, "so that she may not wear me out by continually coming" does not capture the full force of the verb *hypopiazein*. It is a boxing term (see 1 Corinthians 9:26-27) that means "to blacken the eye." Verse 5 says literally that the judge is afraid the widow will end by blackening his eye!

[5] By Ann M. Heidkamp, in *Women's Prayer Services*, ed. Iben Gjerding and Katherine Kinnamon (Mystic, Conn.: Twenty-Third Publications, 1987), pp. 24-25.

DAY SEVEN
Empowering Spirit

Coming Together in the Spirit

Author Annie Dillard recalls a line of Thomas Merton,
"There is always a temptation to diddle around in the
contemplative life, making itsy-bitsy statues." She reflects
further, "There is always an enormous temptation in all of
life to diddle around making itsy-bitsy friends and meals
and journeys for itsy-bitsy years on end. It is so self-
conscious, so apparently moral, simply to step aside from
the gaps where the creeks and winds pour down, saying,
I never merited this grace, quite rightly, and then to sulk
along the rest of your days on the edge of rage. I won't
have it. The world is wilder than that in all directions,
more dangerous and bitter, more extravagant and bright.
We are making hay when we should be making whoopee;
we are raising tomatoes when we should be raising Cain,
or Lazarus."[1]

Defining Our Thematic Context

When we step out on the Word of God, we may,
indeed, be tempted to take only itsy-bitsy baby steps
when God is asking for a leap of faith. What gives us
confidence to take such strides is when we let ourselves

be found by God whose extravagant love finds us, no matter how lost we are. In kind, we can fling ourselves with abandon into the arms of God's love in our constant prayer. We loosen our grip on our material goods as we stretch our grasp toward the treasure God has in store for us. We let subversive seeds take root in us as we become parabolic preachers. We dine in God's realm, not knowing who will be coming to dinner, yet ready to welcome all. We choose the side of the voiceless and the poor as we persist in our pursuit of justice. No half-way measures are adequate when we become immersed in this life of discipleship. There is no tameness to what God offers. The Spirit helps us, plunges us into God, draws us to the Crucified One, and impels us to live and proclaim Christ's liberating message.

Opening Prayer

> Fiery Spirit
> Fount of Courage
> life within life
> of all that has being
>
> O sacred breath
> O Blazing love
> O Savior in the breast and balm
> flooding the heart with
> the fragrance of good,
>
> O limpid mirror of God
> who leads wanderers home and hunts out the lost,
>
> O current of power permeating all
> in the heights upon the earth
> and in all deeps:

you bind and gather
all people together.

Out of you clouds
come streaming, winds
take wing from you, dashing
rain against stone;
and ever-fresh springs well from you, washing
the evergreen globe.

O teacher of those who know,
a joy to the wise
is the breath of Sophia.

Praise then be yours!
You are the song of praise,
the delight of life,
a hope and potent honor
granting garlands of light.[2]

Retreat Session Seven

Listen as Jesus speaks:

There is so much more I want to share with you, dear retreatant, than seven days allow. Just as there was so much more I wanted to teach those who were with me in my earthly ministry. They followed me all the way to my death in Jerusalem. They struggled and were afraid, but so was I in those last days in the Holy City.

I already told you about our last meal together. Afterward we went out across the Kidron Valley to Gethsemane, where we had met many times. I had a great sense of foreboding. I thought this might be our last night together. As I began to pray, I asked my disciples to pray too, that they may not undergo the test (Luke 22:40). I began to plead with God to let this cup pass from me (22:42). But as always, I prayed to know and follow God's will. I remembered that powerful time of prayer on the mountain when I understood that my own death would not be the end of everything, but rather, the new way to liberation for God's people (9:28-36). I clung to that graced moment and begged God to give me the strength to go through with it.

It would be so easy to slip over the other side of the Mount of Olives and into the Judean desert—they would never find me there. But then how would God's will be done? I remembered my mother telling me how hard it was for her to understand God's ways. And how she had taught me to pray, "I am the servant of God; let it be done to me according to your will." She had spoken to me of how God had never let her down, even through her most difficult trials. As I touched into these memories I knew a certain strength and calm, as if God had sent an angel to steel me for the coming ordeal. I knew God was with me and would never abandon me.

When I rose from prayer, I went to my disciples, but they were asleep, poor things. I think they were already grieving. The next moment everything was thrown into chaos. The peaceful garden became awash in torchlight, swords were flying, curses were shouted, and Judas arrived with a murderous crowd. In the confusion somebody cut off the ear of the high priest's servant. I think it was one of my disciples and my heart sank—had they learned so little? I touched the servant's ear and prayed and it was healed (22:50). I looked with love at each of them and prayed that they would recall what I had tried to teach them, "Love your enemies, do good to those who hate you, bless those who curse you, pray for those who mistreat you" (6:27-28).

I wanted them to remember not to return violence with violence—that only fuels the unending spiral of violence. Nor did I want them to be fainthearted. Letting someone walk all over you and abuse you does nothing to stop injustice and oppression. I was trying to show them how to break the cycles of violence and oppression. It would take this one last step on my part to bring it to completion—through death itself.

They took me before the Sanhedrin, our own chief priests and scribes. I knew that what I preached and taught had empowered poor people and undermined the authorities. My hope had been that they would see the light and let go of their false securities and follow me. Still, I continued to pray for them. They were determined to hand me over to Pilate.

Herod was in Jerusalem, too. The two of them had their fun abusing me and making friends at my expense. Eventually Pilate put me before the crowd, and they, too, called for my crucifixion. I don't remember all of the next hours. I think that just as a woman forgets the excruciating pain of giving birth after the joy that floods her when her child is born, so does the agony of my torture and death recede in my memory now that the new life has been opened for God's children.

I remember that throughout I kept praying for a forgiving heart. I was passionately committed to the way God had shown me—the only way to conquer hatred and violence is through forgiving love. I prayed for my disciples, especially Peter. I knew that he would need to know deep forgiving love after the bitter shame of having denied he knew me. I prayed for my torturers, that God would forgive them—how could they know what they were doing? Some of them were just young soldiers who were afraid to do anything but follow orders.

I prayed for the crowd. Many of them had been

carried away by mob mentality. I prayed they would never again find such a spectacle "entertaining." I prayed for the other criminals crucified with me. One of those hanging with me asked if I were not the Messiah and asked me to remember him in my kingdom. He is, indeed, with me now. Then everything went dark and I prayed, "Father, into your hands I commend my spirit" (23:46).

I was very conscious all through my life on earth of being guided by the Spirit. My mother told me that it was by the power of the Holy Spirit that I was conceived and that the Spirit guided her all the time she was pondering God's ways in her heart while she was raising me. I had the same experience from the time that I submitted to John's baptism in the Jordan. While I was praying that day I felt very tangibly the descent of the Spirit on me; it was as if the very heavens opened up and a dove rested upon me. And I heard God's voice telling me how beloved I am and I was flooded with the sense of God's delight in me. A person doesn't forget an experience like that. I returned to it many times in my prayer over the years and it gave me strength and peace in many a difficult moment.

I also knew clearly that this Spirit had not been given me just for my own intimate pleasure with God. I knew that I had been anointed with God's Spirit for mission—a very particular mission to bring glad tidings to the poorest. I had a vision of captive peoples going free, blind people being able to see again, oppressed people liberated from all that held them down—wouldn't God delight with me as together we would bring about such a jubilee time for all! (Luke 4:18-19).

And so it was that as I returned to the Father the last gift I had to hand over, along with my physical life, was this empowering Spirit that guided me throughout my ministry. All was given me as gift and I gratefully handed it back to the Giver.

But that is not the end of the story. You know that the Spirit is still working as powerfully as ever in your own day. My first disciples were so upset and frightened and discouraged after my death. They did not at first understand. They all returned to the upper room in Jerusalem, clinging to memories, trying to sort it all out, and not knowing what to do next. I appeared and spoke to them, explaining as much as I could from the Scriptures, and trying to put them at peace. I told them they would receive power when the Holy Spirit would come upon them and that they would be my witnesses in Jerusalem, throughout Judea and Samaria, and to the ends of the earth (Acts 1:8).

The day of Pentecost they had the kind of experience I had at my baptism, and you should have seen them after that! They were all filled with the Holy Spirit and they began to speak in different tongues and to preach to the people who had gathered in Jerusalem from all parts of the world. They were so enlivened that some scoffers thought they were drunk (Acts 2:13)! They healed people and endured imprisonment and maltreatment—joyfully! All that I showed them, they did exactly.

So, too, dear retreatant, has that power been given to you. On the day of your Baptism you received God's empowering Spirit. In Confirmation it was strengthened in you for mission. You, too, have been given the assurance of God's love and delight to sustain you throughout the most trying times. The Spirit has led you into deserts for testing as it did me (Luke 4:1-13). The Spirit is with you whenever you heal, love and empower God's most needy ones. If there is any doubt in your mind about this, begin one day at a time to take one new step out on the Word of God to live in the forgiving love of the Crucified and Risen One. You can start with itsy-bitsy steps, but before long you should be raising Lazaruses!

There is a Hasidic tale told by Martin Buber that expresses what I mean: "My grandfather was paralyzed. Once he was asked to tell a story about his teacher and he told how the Holy Baal Shem Tov used to jump and dance when he was praying. My grandfather stood up while he was telling the story and the story carried him away so much that he had to jump and dance to show how the master had done it. From that moment, he was healed. This is how stories ought to be told."[3]

This is how the Christian life empowered by the Spirit ought to be lived.

For Reflection

- *How practiced am I in living forgiving love? Is there a first step I can take today to break the cycles of violence and oppression?*

- *Do I remember to pray for those who mistreat me? What effect does it have on cultivating a forgiving heart in me?*

- *Do I claim the power of the Holy Spirit for mission? How does the Spirit enable me to be a healer, reconciler and liberator?*

Closing Prayer

A Spirit Psalm

*(inspired by the image of the Spirit rushing
upon David [1 Samuel 16:13])*

Rush upon us, O Spirit of God!
From this time on, rush upon us
like living water,
like leaping fire,
like fresh breath through an open window.
For this time, rush upon us, O Holy Spirit,
with wisdom and knowledge,
with understanding and counsel,
with wonder and recognition and awe.
Just in time, rush upon us, O Spirit of God,
in life-giving words,
in songs from the voiceless,
in a passion for witness.
At this time, rush upon us, O Holy Spirit,
this hopeful time,
this searching time,
this preparing time,
this coming and going time,
this trusting time,
this new time,
this full time.
All the time,
Rush upon us, O Spirit of God![4]

Notes

[1] Annie Dillard, *Pilgrim at Tinker Creek* (New York: Harper & Row, 1974), p. 268.

[2] By Hildegard of Bingen in Gloria Durka, *Praying with Hildegard of Bingen* (Winona, Minn.: St. Mary's Press, 1991).

[3] A Hasidic tale told by Martin Buber, passed on by John Shea in *Stories of God* (Chicago: Thomas More, 1978), p. 67.

[4] Composed by Rev. Joseph Fortuna for the Cardinal Suenens Symposium May 31-June 3, 1996, sponsored by John Carroll University, Cleveland, Ohio.

Going Forth to Live the Theme

This retreat has highlighted only some of the many traditions about Jesus that I have preserved in my Gospel. Elizabeth, Mary and Jesus have taught us about praying always. The stories of the lost and found sheep, coin and son have invited us to accept God's costly love. Peter, who left everything behind to fish for people, Mary Magdalene, who used her wealth to finance Jesus' mission, and the disciples in Acts who shared all things in common, showed us the many ways one can respond to Jesus' invitation to discipleship.

The subversive seed parables introduced us to Jesus' radical teaching that can turn the world upside down—if we let it! Dangerous dinners with people like Levi, the loving woman who had been a sinner, and the last supper, led us to ponder how inclusive our meal gatherings are. The stories of Mary and Martha, the woman healed of her bent back to glorify God, and the widow persistently pursuing justice immersed us in questions of gender equality. What would it mean today to "choose the better part?" And finally, we claimed the power of the Spirit that has been given each of us in Baptism.

But there is so much more we have left unsaid. There are many other important characters in my Gospel that we did not have time to hear from in this retreat. And there are many other important themes in my Gospel that we have not had time to explore more deeply. So I invite you at the end of this retreat, to consider reading the whole of my Gospel and reflecting on it piece by piece over the next several months.

Let each character come to life for you. Try to put yourself in their shoes and encounter Jesus as they did. Begin each new day with a prayer to have the courage to step out on the Word of God in whatever way God is asking you this day. That is how the good news is witnessed "to the ends of the earth" (Acts 1:8)!

Deepening Your Acquaintance

Books and Commentaries

Bailey, Kenneth E. *Poet & Peasant and Through Peasant Eyes. A Literary-Cultural Approach to the Parables in Luke*, 2 vols. in 1. Grand Rapids, Mich.: Eerdmans, 1976.

Fitzmyer, Joseph A. *The Gospel According to Luke*, 2 vols., Anchor Bible 28-28A. Garden City, N.Y.: Doubleday, 1981, 1985.

Green, Barbara. *Like a Tree Planted: An Exploration of Psalms and Parables Through Metaphor.* Collegeville: Minn.: The Liturgical Press, 1997.

Johnson, Luke T. *The Gospel of Luke*, Sacra Pagina 3. Collegeville, Minn.: The Liturgical Press, 1991.

LaVerdiere, Eugene. *Dining in the Kingdom of God: The Origins of the Eucharist According to Luke.* Chicago: Liturgy Training Publications, 1994.

Reid, Barbara E. *Choosing the Better Part? Women in the Gospel of Luke.* Collegeville, Minn.: The Liturgical Press, 1996.

Ringe, Sharon H. *Luke.* Westminster Bible Companion. Louisville: Westminster/John Knox, 1995.

Schaberg, Jane. "Luke" in *The Women's Bible Commentary*, Carol A. Newsom and Sharon H. Ringe, eds. rev. ed. Louisville, Ky.: Westminster/John Knox, 1998, pp. 363-380.

Seim, Turid Karlsen. "The Gospel of Luke," in *Searching the Scriptures*, Elisabeth Schüssler Fiorenza, ed., Vol. 2. New York: Crossroad, 1994, pp. 728-762.

Senior, Donald. *The Passion of Jesus in the Gospel of Luke*, Wilmington, Del.: Glazier, 1989.

Talbert, Charles H. *Reading Luke: A Literary and Theological Commentary on the Third Gospel*. New York: Crossroad, 1988.

Audiocassette

Reid, Barbara E. *Women in the Gospel of Luke*. Cincinnati: St. Anthony Messenger Press.